Winning the Battle for Attention:

Internet Marketing for Small Business

STUART ATKINS

Copyright © 2015 Stuart Atkins
All rights reserved.

ISBN: 1503128628
ISBN 13: 9781503128620

Soli Deo gloria

Illustrations by Jamie Lee Sugarman

a process based on a few simple platforms, plug-ins, concepts, and hard work. It was hard work that worked. It was also hard work that landed me new clients.

As important as social media is in the world of Facebook, LinkedIn, Twitter, and all the other social "flavors of the month," if your website is not the foundation of your digital strategy, then you're making a big mistake. All social and digital roads lead to your website. Remember: you don't own your Facebook account, your Twitter account, or your LinkedIn account. In fact, you don't own any of your social media accounts—the social media companies do. Through no fault of your own, your account could get hacked or shut down. If you're basing your business success and communication on such social tools, you're in big trouble.

But remember what you *do* own: your website. You own the legal rights to your domain name, and—most importantly—you own and control your website content. It's all yours. As they say, possession is nine-tenths of the law. In the digital world, it is the law. Your website is the foundation of your digital strategy. Your website, not social media, is the best conversion platform. Never forget this.[1]

Sometimes you'll notice repeated principles and best practices in this book. It's intentional because we have short memories. I do. We all suffer from digital amnesia. Forgive me, but there is a method to my occasionally repetitive madness.

---

1 Shama Hyder Kabani, *The Zen of Social Media Marketing* (Dallas: Benbella Books, Inc., 2010), 11.

So what follows is a practical, action-oriented guide to what I learned during my company's Internet journey. I've made mistakes, and I'm still learning. Any errors simply mean that I'm human. What you'll read works as long as you work. Enjoy the read.

Stuart Atkins
Orange, California

ACKNOWLEDGMENTS

Without the help of the following people, this book would not have been possible. Immense thanks go to my wife, Pam—your continued support and patience with my entrepreneurial ventures is forever appreciated. You "went with the flow" as I started Atkins Marketing Solutions, and for that I'm grateful and will love you always. To my adult kids—Celeste, Keane, and Gabe—thanks for your endless support and laughter and for tolerating and loving your random dad. Thanks also go to my late great-grandfather, Elias C. Atkins, founder of the Atkins Saw Company, whom I "met" through a historical journey to his Montana past, compliments of Jacoby Lowney; my dad, Henry, and my mom, Mabel, whom I miss; my sisters, Edie and Linda, who always cheer me on to yet another book and challenge; my brother, Jon, who not only loves to talk business but also keeps me honest as a Colts fan; my sister-in-law, Bev, who is always a source of encouragement, plus a great sounding board, and her husband, Russ, for CPA "on-call" advice; my mother-in-law, Norma, who lets me call her "Mom"; my brother-in-law, Dave, who still likes my golf swing; Dr. Irene Lange, who continues to encourage my teaching at Cal State Fullerton; all the faculty at the Mihaylo College of Business and Economics marketing department; Dr. Neil Granitz, who offered invaluable and detailed feedback on this manuscript; Dr. Steven Chen, who also offered feedback on this book; Dr. Anil Puri, Dean of the Mihaylo College of Business and Economics, for his leadership and encouragement; John Jackson, for his manuscript input and support; Dr. Bill Paulin, my former Pepperdine professor, for his friendship, business and consulting advice; Seth Godin, for permission to use his classic blog post about selling online; Bob Bly for his support and insights on writing, marketing, and selecting the right clients; my marketing assistant and former student, Kari Sugarman, who has been a remarkable source of professionalism, kindness, and support for both my business and this book; Jamie Sugarman, for her illustrations that added fun and creative imagery to this book; all of my clients and their stories that have touched my life and business over the years, thank you for letting me serve you; David Wu, for the opportunity to be a part of your US market vision; Pat Hurley, for your edits and friendship; Dr. Eisenbach Senior, for the honor its been to help your practice; Dr. Eisenbach Jr., for the referral to your dad and the opportunity to consult on your projects, too; Kelly Flint of Constant Contact and your continued support, patience, and encouragement of my skills and business; Corissa St. Laurent of Constant Contact and your patience, understanding, and support; all ALEs in the Southern California Constant Contact team; everyone at the Constant Contact HQ and their fantastic support and help; Mike Daniel, Director of the Long Beach SBDC and all of the remarkable staff I worked with and small businesses I advised; all the wounded and fallen warriors of the US military and their families—thank you for your service and sacrifice on the altar of freedom; all those with Tourette's who work, live, and survive in spite of our challenges; and all of my university students who have enriched my life and allowed me to bring the real world to their lives, careers, and classrooms.

Chapter 1

THE POWER OF A THOUGHTFUL WEBSITE

"We live, for the first time in history, in a world where being part of a globally interconnected group is the normal case for most citizens."—Clay Shirky[1]

Since its commercial inception in 1995, the Internet has not stopped growing. It just can't contain itself. People, businesses, nonprofits, organizations, universities, institutions, and governments use the Internet. It has no boundaries.

Here are some key growth facts:

- Over three billion people worldwide use the Internet. That's roughly 42 percent of the world's population.[2]

---

1 Clay Shirky, *Cognitive Surplus: Creativity and Generosity in a Connected Age* (New York: Penguin Press, 2010), 23–24.

2 http://Internetworldstats.com

- From 2000 to 2014 alone, the Internet grew over 741 percent worldwide.[3]
- In Africa, Internet usage grew over 6,500 percent from 2000 to 2014.[4]
- It's growing right now as I write this bullet point.

There is still room for massive growth. Less than 60 percent of the world's population does not yet have Internet access. The penetration in North America is now over 87 percent.[5] Thus, the continued growth of the Internet is a given. The stats are impressive and create the "wow" factor. However, just because the macro-Internet is growing does not mean your micro-Internet site traffic will grow or that your business will grow. Why? Because not just any website will do. You have to invest the time, effort, money, thought, and learning to attract targeted and relevant visitors. Notice I say "relevant" visitors. Any visitor will not do. You need visitors who match what your business offers.

Because there are so many websites, yours has to be better. Competition means scrutiny. Since the sheer number of websites has increased, the number of bad websites has also increased. Be a good—not a bad—website. Get found.

Will a website really make a difference for your business? Will it really drive both traffic and sales for your small business? The answer is yes, but not just any site will do. Your site has to include specific elements and attributes. The right website needs the "right stuff." Without this, you may have a mild online presence that creates an

3 Ibid.
4 Ibid.
5 Ibid.

occasional visit or phone call, or perhaps even some sales. But a site that cuts through the clutter and creates a consistent brand presence is a different matter. Yet all too often I meet small business clients who simply threw their site up with little thought or reflection. Digital presence does not guarantee financial profit.

Ultimately, you owe your visitors and customers some thought—digital thought. You need to earn their visit and business, and that takes work. In fact, a site that fits your target visitors saves them money while making you money. Seth Godin hits the digital nail on the head when he says that you must answer one critical question when a person visits your site: "Why am I here?"[6]

A thoughtful website can do wonders for your business.[7] I say "thoughtful" because your business probably already has a website. However, what kind of site is it? Perhaps a few pictures, static pages, and a phone number? Maybe more, maybe less. But the real question is, "When was the last time you really thought about your website?" When was the last time you audited your website? When was the last time you took a serious look at what visitors do when they arrive at your website?

A great website will give your company the following benefits.

Showcase competitive advantage

The fundamental basis to both good marketing and a successful business is competitive advantage. Your product must be

---

6 http://sethgodin.typepad.com/seths_blog/2013/07/qa-what-works-for-websites-today.html

7 http://searchenginewatch.com/article/2293329/Its-Time-to-Update-the-Definition-of-a-Website

different to be better. Your product must step outside of the commodity category and into the custom solution. The legendary marketing guru and professor, Dr. Phillip Kotler, says that "competitive advantage is a company's ability to perform in one or more ways that competitors cannot or will not match."[8]

Because in all industries there are competitors, there will also be websites that showcase and define those competitors. Your competitors will have websites. Some will be better than others, and some will be better than yours. Don't let that happen. A good website is one of the best ways to clearly communicate what makes your products unique, different, and better. How your website performs relative to your competition should express your competitive advantage. You may have the most unique products around, but if a website visitor finds your competitor's site before yours, you're at a disadvantage.

Just like large corporations, small businesses can differentiate their products by form, features, customization, performance quality, durability, reliability, reparability, and style.[9] If your small business is service oriented, you can set yourself apart through ordering ease, delivery, installation, customer training, customer consulting, and maintenance and repair.

A good website can showcase both product and service differentiators. All of the differentiator characteristics just mentioned are easily communicated on a website. In fact, it's especially effective if your past and current customers do the talking through

---

8 Philip Kotler and Kevin Lane Keller, *Marketing Management* (14th ed.) (Upper Saddle River, NJ: Prentice Hall, 2012), 289.

9 Ibid., 329–30.

videos, testimonials, and reviews of your products and services that are easily accessible on your website.

In short, competitive advantage must be communicated to be an advantage. Few tools do this better than a website, especially a good website. Consequently, if you have great products but a poor website, you're hiding or eroding your competitive advantages. Make sure your website adds value for your customers and not for your competition. Much of what follows in this book will do just that.

From owning a business to creating brand awareness

Just because you own a business does not mean you own a brand. A business exists from the start but a brand takes times to build. Over time, you build a bridge from your business to your customer through your brand. The Nike checkmark logo took time to grow from an unrecognizable symbol to a household name.

In essence, a brand is a promise. Your potential customer needs a solution and your product promises to provide that solution. Yet a brand goes far beyond just a logo or a tag line or a name. A good brand has consistency of color, design, and, most importantly, messaging. You have to tell your story and the story can't be told unless you spread the word. A good website spreads the word like no other tool because you don't have to shout to get people's attention. They search and find you rather than you shouting to get their attention. Often, customers find you before you find them. How? Through search—Internet search.

In many cases, people find companies and products by a simple Internet search. They type in a keyword and phrase, hit **Enter**, and your home page does the rest, provided you apply the remaining chapters in this book. If your site is visible and has caught the attention of the major search engines, chances are a potential customer may become aware of your brand and company simply through such a search. Some of my best clients, speaking gigs, and radio interviews found me from my website. I did not seek them. If your website is search friendly (a topic I cover in later chapters), your brand will be friendly. If people can't find you online, they don't know you exist. Scary but true. Awareness of your brand is often dependent on your website's visibility. If your website is not on the radar, your brand won't be either. If a potential customer can't find you, how can that person buy from you? Let yourself be found.

Establish credibility

Credibility creates sales. Your website is the digital first impression to your business. Your website introduces you to a person who has never met you in person. Thus, first impressions matter. Once a new site visitor lands on your site, you have roughly ten seconds to grab that person's attention. Make your case fast. You must let it be known that you're a credible, professional, benefit-oriented source for what that person wants. It could be information, or your product, or both.

To establish credibility, your site will need a good home page that quickly tells what your company does and how you can benefit the visitor. Your About Us page and your blog will be the two key credibility factors. Your About Us page gives your bio and background.

Your blog proves you know what you're talking about. It gives you the opportunity to show your thought leadership.

Credibility keeps first-time visitors on your site. It helps them stick around for a few more minutes, which is critical. Don't give a new visitor a reason to leave your home page. Be credible.

If by chance you don't have a website, well, your competition is thanking you. If potential customers search for your business online and find no website, your credibility is immediately tarnished. If they have a choice between a company that has a website versus one that does not, which do you think they'll pick? You'll be ignored. No information and no online presence is bad presence. Your business has to show up. No site, no chance at either credibility or success.

Establish your thought leadership

I already touched on thought leadership. Let me elaborate. Thought leadership is important because customers and clients like businesses that know what they're talking about. Chances are you know your product better than anybody. You are the expert. Give examples, case studies, stories, client testimonies, and tips that prove your thought leadership. Show how your approach sets you apart.

I often tell prospective clients to look at my blog posts. These posts stand as a historical legacy and journal of how I approach marketing. If I can't think for myself, how can I think for my clients? The creation of your own content sets you apart from your competition.

In this age of expert pretenders, you need to prove your digital worth. Your website can do this, especially if you generate your own content. Original content shows original thinking. So before you hire any consultants with your hard-earned money, look at their thought leadership via their websites.

Work while you sleep

A good website is a 24/7 sales engine. It sells while you snore. No other marketing tool works nonstop like a website. It never tires, sleeps, or gets sick. It's always on call and ready to sell your product or service. It knows no time-zone limitations and will sell your product at any time to anyone.

The reward with such effort is gold. In fact, knowing your objective actually makes site design easier. It gives you a road map and focal point. Design for design's sake leads to visitor confusion. Design based on a strategic objective creates visitor delight. It actually makes a visit fun. Visitors find you, get what they need, buy, learn something during the visit, and then hopefully bookmark and return.

Creating objectives

To create your site objectives, do three things. Envision the persona of your typical site visitor, or target customer, and ask the following questions:

1. "Why does my website exist?"
2. "Why would visitors come to my site?"
3. "What's the purpose of my website?"[14]

14 Roberts and Zahay, *Internet Marketing: Integrating Online & Offline Strategies* (Madison, OH: South-Western, 2013), 60.

As for questions one and two, below is a list of possible site visits. Woody Allen once said, "Eighty percent of success is showing up." That may be true in life, but with a website, mere arrival does not guarantee success. Visitors are there for a reason. They want to do something. So why did they show up for a digital visit? Here are a few possible reasons:

- I'm bored.
- I found this site by accident.
- I'm looking for your expertise.
- I need help in your product or service category.
- I'm a hacker.
- I'm a spammer.
- I make "money" by bothering websites.
- I'm a bot bum and have nothing better to do.
- I need to do something.
- My business is suffering.
- I need to see what my competition is up to.
- I like good content.
- I typed in a question on Google.
- I like to learn.
- I need to buy a service or a product.
- I need information.
- I need to grow sales.
- I need to understand my customers.
- I don't know.
- I sell links.
- I steal others' content without permission.
- I know you.
- I heard you speak.
- I read your book.
- I took your class.
- I need marketing help.
- You fill in the blank:

____

What's a persona?

A persona is a basic profile that characterizes the lifestyle of various individuals. It's a target market personified. It could be soccer moms, football fans, weekend warriors, tech geeks, bikers, do it yourselfers, tattoo lovers, bird watchers. You name it and there is often a persona or psychographic category you place a customer in, based on that customer's lifestyle, sense of self, convictions, values, and what they like to do when they're not working. In short: spare-time passions. Think of a magazine rack and you have personas or target markets for each magazine category. Many customers may buy magazines, but only specific ones buy *National Geographic, Time, Guns & Ammo,* or *Bride* magazine. The magazine category is a name tag called "persona."

Website usability expert, Jakob Nielsen, explains the persona concept well:

> A persona is a fictional character representative of a unique group of users who share common goals. An organization should possess several personas to reflect the variety of visitors that its website attracts (most commonly, three to seven personas will cover the majority of an audience without creating too specific or spurious distinctions in your user types). These user archetypes should ideally be based on qualitative, ethnographic user research in order to include accurate behaviors, environments, attitudes, and needs of real users. Personal details such as a name, photo, and specific contextual narratives should be combined

> with a description of gender, age, marital status, job title, device ownership, and other demographic information to create an easy-to-imagine, relatable character.[15]

Here are some additional tips to find personas:

- Create a profile for your ideal customer. Who frequently buys that product or service?
- Describe this customer in persona terms: Joe the Plumber; Yuppie Geek; Working Mom; Soccer Mom; Busy Professional; Active Senior; NASCAR Dad; Football Freak; Food Fanatic; Motorcycle Mike; Small Business Sammy. You get the idea. The persona is the descriptive metaphor in two or three words. Say the phrase and the image pops up.
- Be careful not to stereotype.
- Work from general to specific. For example, start with teachers, online teachers, online teachers working part-time, and online teachers working part-time in California.
- Don't forget: the wider your message, the greater the chance a potential customer will receive it as spam. Being more specific means a lower bounce rate (visitors who leave your site quickly after viewing only one page). Target, don't tease.

---

15 http://www.nngroup.com/articles/analytics-persona-segment/?utm_source=Alertbox&utm_campaign=d2d8c53055-Segment_Analytics_Personas_12_01_2014&utm_medium=email&utm_term=0_7f29a2b335-d2d8c53055-24074673

- Then start focusing your messaging, words, concepts, ads, images, promotions, and content to fit that persona and what makes it tick.
- Don't just broadcast—listen to social media. There are lots of social personas in the digital world we often miss because we don't listen to concerns, trends, complaints, and requests. Listen carefully.

Ultimately, if you decrease the distance between a potential visitor's keyboard and your website, you've met one critical objective: they can find you. Furthermore, by matching your target persona to your products or services, you significantly increase the odds for getting an engaged visitor. You're offering solutions that fit—engaging solutions that solve problems and create sales. You're meeting needs and not forcing a spam-filled interruption. It's that simple and yet that hard. It takes time, attention, and effort.

Objectives are prime. No objectives equal a confused visitor.

Visitors don't buy what they don't understand. Help them turn a *why* into a *buy*.

Questions and action items

1. What's the main objective of your website?
2. Why do visitors come to your site?
3. Describe, in detail, the typical persona you want visiting your website.

4. Are there multiple customer personas you may be targeting?
5. What do you want visitors to do when they arrive at your site?
6. Does your home page confuse a new visitor?
7. Ask fifteen people to visit your home page. What feedback did they give you?

Chapter 3

WHAT THE FACEBOOK ARE YOU TRYING TO SAY?

"Speak clearly, if you speak at all; carve every word before you let it fall."—Oliver Wendell Holmes Sr.

Without a doubt, one of the leading problems I see with websites is messaging. It never fails. Time after time, the home page leaves me with one question: "What are you trying to say?" I enter the domain name, hit **Enter**, land on the home page, and ponder what I found. I'm just not sure who you are, what you do, and what you're telling and selling me. For a second, I sometimes think I've landed on a Greek, French, or German foreign language page. Then I see it's English, yet I need a translator to understand the message. Not good. I leave.

Have you ever felt that way while visiting a website?

A clear and simple message keeps visitors on the page. Simplicity is what you owe your visitors. Make the visit easy. Effort often means they leave, or better said in analytic, metric-linguistic, etymological-digital-semantic-stochastic-epistemological terms: a bounce. They view the page, get confused, and leave. Yes, the fancy words were intentional. Don't get fancy. I know, you almost skipped to Chapter 4 because of it.

Here are some leading message profiles I often see.

Nothing

Yes, that's correct: nothing. Some websites, even though they have text, say nothing. Either the content makes no sense at all, or it makes too much sense. For example, this past week I met with a client who owns an established research company. It had great success in the past, yet, due to increased competition through online options, it is faced with rebranding and reworking the messaging. I went to its website. It sounded good but I just couldn't understand what the company did. The "So what?" question was not answered. The "I have no idea" question was answered.

Say something. Make every word count. A visitor's time is valuable and you need to make it count. Saying "something" can sometimes mean nothing. Beware the temptation to use filler—content that uses industry or marketing speak. Catchwords and phrases taken from corporate-speak copy mean little to a site visitor who needs your help.

of this. If your content scored between ninety to one hundred, your writing was easily understood by an average fifth grader. Scores between sixty to seventy were easily understood by the average eighth and ninth grader, and scores between zero and thirty were easily understood by the average college graduate.

The scale is not perfect. There are some subjective elements and ambiguities that make it open to interpretation by both writer and reader. However, it at least gives you a fair indication of which target age and audience will understand your writing. In fact, some of the best SEO plug-ins available today for WordPress use the Flesch scale to assist with content SEO and SEM analysis. If you target the ten-year-old level, you'll often find your content resting in the sixty to seventy range.

As I said earlier, this is not meant to make your web copy childish. Instead, it actually does the reader a favor. They can quickly understand your message. No confusion. Site visitors like simple because it eliminates confusion. It's hard on your end but easy on the reader's end. You really have to write simply, but the end result creates an improved visitor reading experience. Make the page visit enjoyable, not an exercise in philosophical contemplation.

Make sure your site visitor does not have to work to translate your site message. If your message is not clear in five to ten seconds, at most, that visitor will leave and become a statistical bounce to your website. A bounce is simply this: the visitor lands, looks, and leaves if it does not make sense.

Your value proposition

If I could give a small business one tip for its website, it's this: include a value proposition in the first paragraph on the home page. "What's a value proposition?" you may ask. In short, it defines in one sentence why a customer should buy from you. It's like the opening line of a play. A good value proposition sets the stage for your website audience. For example, my website home page leads with the following value proposition: "We help you audit your marketing, tell your story, and find your customer."

Boom. Done. Simple, short, to the point. No confusion. It may not be perfect but it accomplishes its purpose. If you hire me as a consultant, I will assess your marketing and make sure you tell a story that resonates with your target customer. As a result of a refined marketing strategy and story, finding your customer is much easier. In the time it takes to read this opening value proposition, a new site visitor knows what they're getting into. It's clear and to the point. In addition, I used to include, "Atkins Marketing Solutions is a small business marketing consulting company." This was the first of two sentences encompassing the value proposition. I then realized that users would see the "Atkins Marketing Solutions" name in the masthead (image or brand logo in the top of a website), and URL of the website, so why be redundant? I decided to get directly to the point in one sentence.

Your benefits list

After your value proposition, a benefits list is also a welcome element to most home pages. The value proposition tells visitors why they should buy and the benefits list tells them what you'll do for them. It answers the "So what?" question. Furthermore, it's best to use bullet points when listing your top benefits. You can also add a hybrid form of your benefits list to your services page. Placing benefits on both the home page and your services page is best, thus covering two key pages on your digital real estate.

I recommend listing your top three to five benefits. You may have more, but if you had to pick three to five, which would they be? If you struggle choosing the top three to five, think about what your customers have told you. Sift through past reviews and testimonials. You'll see the common benefits. Use them. If these benefits generated past revenue, chances are they'll generate future revenue. They're proven and tested, so list them in a short, simple benefits list.

Using bullet points also forces you to encapsulate the guts of what will help the customer. I often call bullet points the ammunition of brevity. They're perfect for the online page since we read 25 percent slower online than on paper.[18] A list of bullet points can paint a picture of a thousand words. In fact, a single, good bullet point can sometimes communicate more than an entire paragraph.

Remember, a website home page with both an effective value proposition and benefits list goes a long way. In some cases, these messaging elements are all you need on most home pages. It's fundamental and core. Subsequently, these elements alone may generate a call or an e-mail. They also serve to guide and direct other messaging tools, both traditional and digital.

18 http://www.nngroup.com/articles/be-succinct-writing-for-the-web

Value and benefits give your home page a focal point. It's the lighthouse that shows visitors where they're going and how you can get them there. In the storms of Internet messaging and communication, make sure you help your visitors navigate toward understanding.

Questions and action items

1. Cut and paste your home page content into the Flesch Reading scale. What's your level?
2. Ask a real ten-year-old to read your page copy. Do they understand?
3. Reduce your home page text by 50 percent. Is any verbal furniture left? Is every word necessary?
4. Do you have a value proposition on your home page? If not, write one.
5. Do you have a benefits list on your home page? If not, write one.
6. Have a ten-year-old read both your value proposition and benefits statement. Do they get it?

Chapter 4

SEO: FROM CONVERSATION TO CONVERSION

"Content is king, but marketing is queen, and runs the household."—Gary Vaynerchuk

All the chapters in this book are important, but this one may top them all. If your website gets SEO right, magic and revenue often fall into place. No other topic is more needed yet more misunderstood. The vast number of snake-oil SEO companies in existence often prey on unsuspecting and unaware victims. It's key that you understand the basics of what to do and what not to do, and what to watch out for. Without some basic SEO education, you may throw money out your digital window with little result.

I often get e-mails from SEO companies claiming they can "Launch your website to the top of Google's page rank." Such e-mails also list a series of SEO shortcomings on your site related to links, keywords, and numerous other faults. These companies take advantage of people's insecurities and lack of SEO knowledge to drive a sale. In fact, my website's the Alexa ranking is often better than these SEO companies. Some even have the nerve to send an e-mail from Gmail. Come on. If you're a real company, why not send an e-mail from a domain I can check? My advice: ignore them. Delete those e-mails.

Do some basic, organic SEO work on your site. It's not rocket science but it's work. Many small businesses are not prepared or motivated to do the work. Do some work first and generate some revenue that may later pay for legitimate SEO service providers. Also, the efforts associated with learning organic SEO principles will leave you better prepared if you do later hire a legitimate SEO company. There are some good and reputable SEO companies out there in "cyberspace." Note: the good ones are usually not cheap. You will pay starting around $500 per month. But once a site has the foundational search engine friendliness and basic SEO in place, a good SEO company might be worth it.

Let's define two key phrases: SEO and SEM.

What's SEO?

SEO, or search engine optimization, covers the fundamental building blocks a website needs to keep Google happy. By Google, I also mean all the major search engines, such as Ask, Bing, and Yahoo. Like a house foundation, the stronger the foundation the stronger the house. With a website, the stronger the "marketing consultant," "marketing services," "Internet marketing," and "small business marketing," to name just a few. Since search engines know and track the keyword phrases that are typed for given businesses, including the right phrases in your page content is critical.

To find what the most popular keywords are, look at some of your competitors' sites. You can also find a goldmine of keywords by using PPC advertising offered by Google, Bing, and Yahoo. The chapter on PPC covers this in more detail. Another great way to find great keywords is through your analytics tools, such as Google Analytics. These tools will list the daily keywords, or search terms, visitors used to find your website. Some of those terms are random and some are relevant.

The chapter on blogging also talks about the consistent and fresh content needed to get the attention of search engines when they scan your website. All the organic, on-site content included in your website is the other side of the attention coin. To win the battle for attention, your site must have quality and relevant, organic keywords and phrases included on your pages.

Good SEO is just good marketing

SEO is not rocket science. It actually existed well before the Internet was invented. "What do you mean?" you ask. It's simple: marketing. Yes, marketing. The tried and true principles of marketing fit perfectly with SEO. Marketing is Queen to the King called SEO.

Good marketing

- Thinks customer before product.
- Has a target or group of people in mind rather than selling to the entire world.
- Concentrates on a message that the customer understands.
- Advertises in a consistent, integrated fashion.
- Provides value in the form of quality content and information the customer can use, often for free.
- Listens rather than interrupts.
- Has a mission statement.
- Runs on objectives, not guesses.
- Looks at the internal strengths of a business.
- Looks at the internal weaknesses of a business.
- Looks at the external opportunities of a market.
- Looks at the external threats of a market.
- Looks at the numbers.
- Has a strategy.
- Looks at the product, price, place, and promotion where the product is sold.
- Executes, assesses, and then makes changes to move forward.

Some quick best practice SEO tips

I significantly improved my website visibility by applying the following tips, and increased my site traffic by gradually implementing these practices. I'm not so much interested in a search engine ranking as I am seeing a consistent, growing trend of both new and returning relevant traffic to my website.[21]

Here are the goods—a quick list on how to get started on your own site SEO:

- Use WordPress. Period. Let me say it again: use WordPress for your website. It's not just a content management and blogging platform anymore. WordPress does it all.
- Include a blog as part of your site. An integrated blog ensures your website reaps the benefits of regular content updates. Unlike any other addition to your website, an integrated blog increases the organic strength and search engine ranking of your site. If your blog is a separate domain outside of your website, you're competing against yourself.
- Post two to four times per month.
- Post relevant content that relates directly to your business and area of expertise.
- Make your posts benefit-oriented, with tips and practical info to help your readers.
- Use an SEO plug-in, such as WordPress SEO by Yoast, to filter and improve each page and post.

21 www.AtkinsMarketingSolutions.com

- Do keyword research and integrate those leading terms and phrases into your page copy. Write in a natural, not mechanical style.
- Use Google AdWords and learn from your keyword research.
- Use custom descriptions for each page of your site. Match the page title to the focus content of each page.
- Link Facebook and Twitter posts back to your blog using a social media share bar with each post. There are plenty of good share bar plug-ins for WordPress.
- Use the Alexa toolbar. Go to Alexa.com to see what's available and where your site ranks. It will be an eye opener the first time you enter your URL and hit **Enter**.
- Get your blog listed on Technorati.
- Get your site URL listed on as many relevant websites as possible. The better the external links returning to your site the better your site visibility and credibility with search engines.
- Watch your page load speed. The slower the page load speed the higher the abandonment rate. Check this speed at pingdom.com, gtmetrix.com, and webpagetest.org.
- Be patient. It takes time for the major search engines to trust you, often three to twelve months.
- Register your domain name for at least five to ten years rather than the typical annual renewal. This shows major search engines your domain commitment is long-term and serious.
- Don't overdesign your site. Google likes sites that offer relevant content, not digital art museums that dance around like the Disneyland night parade. Again, relevant content beats fancy design any day.

- Use AWSTATS and Google Analytics to track your site traffic and progress. If you don't check what's happening with your site numbers, you're flying blind. Don't fly blind.

These are just a few of my tips. Apply the above and you'll both save money and increase relevant traffic to your website. They're not a substitute for pure SEO practices but they are a foundation if you later decide to invest funds with a credible SEO company. Make sure your site is at least search engine friendly before investing in further SEO services. The preceding recommendations will help you move in that direction.

Questions and action items

1. How fast, or slow, is your website?
2. How often do you update your site content?
3. Do you know how many visitors come to your site daily?
4. Do you know where they come from?
5. Is your domain registration one year or five to ten years?
6. What's your Alexa ranking?
7. How many external, credible websites link back to your site?
8. Do you know what your top five keywords or phrases are for your website?
9. Have you looked at some of your competitors' websites to find possible keywords?
10. Are your leading keywords included in the first 500 words of your home page?

Chapter 5

CONTENT: IS IT KING AND IS IT SPICY?

"Content is the reason search began in the first place."
—Lee Odden

Is your website royal and spicy? For a good time, should we visit your URL?

No, I don't mean that kind of good time, but nice thought.

With websites, it's often said that content is king. I agree. Without substance, the digital visitor is stuck with fluff—too much text, or verbal furniture. The site content comes across as filler. So keep in mind that your site content's purpose is not to tell your entire life story, nor should it tell your visitors everything about your product and business. It needs to tell enough to make them hungry. Keep them hungry but don't feed them to the point of leaving, barfing, or bouncing from your home page.

Keep in mind that Chapter 3 covered your message. This chapter on content covers the structure and depth of what you say. It also covers how often you say it and the style in which you write it. It's frequency and structure of substance rather than the message. Yes, these topics overlap a bit, but they are different.

Boring substance versus spicy style

The flavor of your website content is important. All too often, site content is corporate and bland, reading like the computerized voicemail recordings we've become so used to: bland, monotone, flat. Boring. And yes, not sexy and fun. It tastes like rice cakes. No spice.

That's right: spicy and fun. How often is what we read simply elevator music and not jammin' rock 'n' roll, hip-hopish, rappy, edgy, and energetic? It may even push the envelope a bit. Judge for yourself from the opening page of two real websites:

Example 1

> We clean all kinds of carpet with the utmost care to meet your standards and to help us achieve our commitment to the level of perfection we put toward our work.
>
> Owner operated since we began serving the local community over ten years ago, The Carpet Care has been known to offer a personal approach to home cleaning that you won't find anywhere else.
>
> The Carpet Care is America's finest carpet cleaning company that offers a complete carpet care solution for people from all walks of life across the country. No carpet is too dirty for us!

The Carpet Care is ready to provide quality cleaning services 'round the clock!

Example 2

Ladies, every revolution begins with a handful of words.

"I have a dream…"
"No, I will not give up my bus seat…"
"Let justice be done though the heavens should fall…"

And those words? They're spoken by a rebel.

Someone who's not cool with the status quo.
Someone who sees a way to make the world better, sooner.
Someone with inner fire, vision, and more creativity than most people know what to do with.
Someone like you.

I'm a rebel who happens to be (radically) gifted with words.
And when I partner with other rebels—'specially women entrepreneurs—things get rowdy.

So here's the deal:

I want to know all about your products, services, retreats, and experiences. Hell, yeah.

> And I want to craft un-frickin'-believable copy to share 'em, sell 'em, and make your rebel bank account very happy.
>
> But most of all?
>
> I want to help you find that handful of words that's gonna set your revolution in motion.
> Your battle cry. Your big WHY. Your "I have a dream..." (Oh, I know you've got one. You ain't shy.)
>
> You in?[22]

Yes, I'm in. So which example hit your fun-and-sexy-factor button? No question. Example 2 is the winner and if you say otherwise, well, I'll refund the money you paid for this book because your site has no hope.

The two copy examples above are night and day cases of turning words into mind magnets versus cooty-infested turn-offs. The first content example is all too common and boring. It's filled with generalizations and commonplace statements that don't grab my attention. I'm sure the carpet cleaners are great people who provide quality service. I'm not trying to knock the business, only the content that describes the business. Can carpet cleaning be fun and sexy? Yes, I bet it can, but you won't find a good time on this website. Or on this carpet? Perhaps this website needs to get a bit dirty, in a good way.

---

22 http://www.nikkigroom.com

As for example two, well, all I can say is I want to meet this woman—I mean business. The content jumps out at me and grabs my laugh-factor, heart, and mind. It draws me in and makes me want to read more. Granted, Nikki Groom, the writer of the copy, is a professional copywriter and a very good one. One of the best.

It may not be a fair comparison but it does make the point: write content that jumps rather than sleeps. Give it some life and give your words some punch. Make them talk so the visitor comes back for more, or at least stays on the page more than ten seconds. See what happens? Just reading her copy makes me write with energy. I need to be reminded of this just as much as you do. We all need to stay away from status quo websites—they don't sell as much as fun, rebel websites.

Be a rebel. Get rowdy. Make the content fun or I'm leaving home—home page, I mean.

Give each page a focus: Home, About Us, Services, Products, Resources, Blog, and Contact Us.

Home Page

There's no place like home page. "Home sweet home page," as a digital Dorothy might say.

The home page is the most important page on any website.[23] In most cases, it's the first page visitors land on—often the only page they land on. It's the starting point for the rest of the site.

23 www.nngroup.com/articles/113-design-guidelines-Homepage-usability

If the home page does not deliver, the visitor leaves. And as I mentioned earlier, if you don't get it right, they may never come back. Ever.

The first three hundred to five hundred words of the home page will set the stage. They make or break whether the visitor stays. It's like a movie trailer, and it better be good. It's the preface, the attention-grabber. The following list includes the must-have elements in a good Homepage:

- Ask yourself, "What's the purpose of this page?" Choose only one purpose.
- State your value proposition in the first paragraph. Better: in the first sentence.
- Include your benefits statement—the top three to five benefits you provide your customers.
- Include a short video telling the story of your business. Two to three minutes max. Professional but casual.
- Some closing content should describe more differentiators about your business. Things that truly set your product apart. What is unique about your product compared to the competition?
- Put your business phone number and e-mail address at the top of the page; make them easily visible.
- Tempt people with links to other pages of your site, or other websites. Keep them on the page and be careful not to include distractions.

Get to the point with short, active (not passive) verb sentences. Don't attempt to include your entire company story or descriptions of all your products or services. Leave that for other pages or blog posts, but please don't flood visitors with information. They can't drink from a fire hose of content. Let them sip.

The home page is the first step in the journey of your site. Make it count. Make your visitors thirsty for more.

About Us

The About Us page tells a story. It's the story of the person or persons behind the business. Because there is often a person behind a product, this page relates the human aspect of your business. People buy from people they connect with, like, and know. Help them to get to know you and your business. Make it a short story. About Us is not about everything.

A good website should be much more about what you can do for the customer than about you. It's them, not you that matters. However, on the About Us page, it's OK to talk about you. Just make sure that *you* relate to *them*. Be human. Tell them the brief history of your business, your background, and why this business matters to both you and the customer. Tell them why you created the business. It could have been by accident, by passion, by necessity, or any number of reasons. Chances are there was a need you saw that matched your background and expertise.

It's best if it's a combination of both a personal and professional history. They key is to make it human. Connect with the customer. Make the biography mean something.

It's also important to briefly list your education, experience, certifications, and other factors that may show your competence. Tell why you are both a thought leader and a solution provider for what they need and you thus provide. A close-up, high-resolution head-shot photo also helps with this important bio page. Don't take a distant, blurry picture with a Sumo wrestler. Make sure it's an engaging facial picture that connects. And if you can swing it, a one- to two-minute video introducing yourself is always a welcome touch. Videos resonate, plus they help people remember you and your business. It's a personal touch that draws people in.

Services

The Services page tells the visitors what you can do for them. It also tells them what you do. Make it results-oriented rather than generic. Including results helps the potential customer connect the business to the benefit. They need solutions and your products or services have to communicate that quickly.

For example, below is a bulleted service list. It's not perfect but you'll get the idea:

- Marketing evaluations resulting in new customers and increased sales.
- Marketing plan development that draws and retains customers.
- E-mail marketing best practices that increase social media followers and brand awareness.
- Social media strategies that target quality rather than just quantity of followers.
- Strategic WordPress advising and planning, resulting in cost-effective and search-friendly websites.
- WordPress content management and creation training.

- Marketing usability advice, resulting in simple and engaging user experiences.
- Content development so website visitors and customers understand your message, connect with your story, and keep returning to your site.
- Google AdWords management that attracts targeted, relevant, and increased traffic to your website.
- Keyword research so Google searches result in increased sales.
- Marketing research that helps you find targeted, buying customers.
- Simple and organic SEO best practices that increase your website traffic.
- Advertising and integrated brand promotion strategies that provide high ROI and maximum reach, frequency, and impact.
- Custom marketing consulting designed to grow your business and retain existing customers.

Note the following words from the preceding list: resulting, draws, retains, attracts, find, increases, provide, and grow. All of these are action-oriented verbs or infinitives. They are "do" words. Action. Move. In short, your business does this so they get that. A plus B = Results.

By briefly listing what they both get and can expect from your company, the page makes it that much easier for the visitor and potential customer to click or call. Put the verbs in your pages. Marketing is a verb. I'm doing verb right now as I write. Every page, every day, little by little, all of us business owners move forward. Make the Services page sing with verbs.

Products

Beware the Product page. It's tricky and must be designed with one concept in mind: usability. Even though I cover this concept in more detail in the next chapter, it has to be touched upon here.

Like all content and copy, Product pages must be simple. The combination of pictures, descriptions, pull-down menus, and **Buy** buttons can lead to either a buy or a bye. The following is an attribute list of what makes a good Product page:

- Bulleted format
- Brief opening and short paragraphs
- Simple product descriptions
- Product benefit listings
- Product feature listings
- Clear call to action

Resources

The Resources page, if you have one, offers free content visitors can download. It includes articles you've written, presentation copies, PDF files, product spec sheets, brochures, white papers, and sometimes even a free e-book you've written.

Make the content on this page a mini-gold mine for visitors. They really appreciate free, usable content that may turn a read into revenue. The key is to keep it updated with regular content—a task that is tough to stay on top of. Perhaps add a new item once per month. Once you establish a respectable library of free content, then update once per month. The key is to make it both regular and current.

Contact Us

The Contact Us page is more for visitor-to-business communication than it is for content. However, in a small but important way, it's information an interested visitor sends to you, the business.

Typically, a good Contact Us page makes it easy for a site visitor to send you a brief message that ends up in your e-mail inbox. Don't be intrusive. Connect. Include the following fill fields:

- First name
- No last name needed
- E-mail address
- Optional phone #
- Comment box for the responder's message
- Say you'll respond in twenty-four to forty-eight hours
- Include both your e-mail address and phone number

Make sure you have at least two individuals who receive these e-mails, so you won't miss a customer's concern or question. You will also get some fantastic leads from your Contact Us page. Test it to ensure it works.

Blog Page

Besides the home page, the blog page makes or breaks your content. If you have a good home page and blog, your site will be effective. The blog is your content generation machine, the repository of your thought leadership, your expertise, your experience. It has the potential to offer the most value to your visitors. Some of my best clients hired me because they read my blog. It also attracts visitors because search engines love blogs. The fresh content attracts their crawlers and as a result improves your website's organic search ranking and viability.

In fact, since the Blog page and its fresh, dynamic content is so important, I've dedicated Chapter 8 to blogging. No other website content page is more important and more neglected than your blog.

For starters, do this:

- To improve organic SEO, integrate your blog as a page on your website. Don't create a separate, stand-alone blog.
- Keep your post titles to seventy characters or less.
- Post at least two times per month. Google loves and notices the fresh, dynamic content. So will your readers.
- Integrate YouTube videos occasionally with your blog posts.
- Integrate e-mail marketing and social media as part of your overall blog and branding strategy.
- Practice comment moderation for your blog, so only the comments you approve are posted. WordPress has powerful filter plug-ins to avoid all comment spam. Use them.
- Approve only value-oriented and thoughtful comments that are specific to your posts.
- Keep your posts focused on your core competencies, subject passion, and expertise.
- Write casually.
- Give credit where credit is due and share your reactions to thought leaders who impact your business and life.
- Include links in posts when relevant.

- Learn, write, contribute, and engage.

Spice. You must have some. Digital spice. Fresh spice. Content cinnamon, natural nutmeg, generous ginger, and powerful, revenue-generating pepper. Good content is the varietal spice of websites. Give each page of your website some kick. Make visitors taste it and come back for more. Make them hungry.

It's fun to eat out. Give your visitors good digital meals. Give them dessert, too.

Make sure they sit down at your website then come back for seconds.

Questions and action items

1. Rank your home page on a scale of one to ten.
2. Does your home page include a value proposition and benefits list?
3. Is there anything on your Homepage that does not need to be there?
4. Reduce your copy density by 50 percent to 70 percent. Reduce more.
5. Do you have a blog?
6. Are you posting at least two to four times per month?

Chapter 6

HEAT MAPS AND USABILITY: WHAT'S HAPPENING ONCE THEY ARRIVE?

"When you go to a site, you usually run into usability problems pretty quickly. They're not hidden. They're not complicated. They're not baffling. They were in the design or crept into the design."—Steve Krug

Have you ever seen a GPS map that tracks your trail? It creates a history of what you've done and where you've been. It's a digital bread-crumb trail that leads you either to revenue or website ruin.

With a website, there are numerous tools to track just what your visitors are doing once they arrive. Heat maps show you where they go, and usability shows just how easy, or hard, it is for them to navigate once they arrive. *Usability* is a fancy term for *user friendly*.

What's a heat map?

A heat map is a graphic visualization of where visitors click and look (eye activity) on a page. It's a hangout map for each specific page of your website. You pick which page or pages you want tracked and you then get, over time, a pattern of behavior about your page activity. Where every visitor clicks is marked in every section of each page. You then glance at a graphic that looks just like each web page, except there are dots and colors that represent specific behaviors and activities.

The heat map company or service provider supplies the HTML code that you simply drop into your website. Within twenty-four hours, you start getting detailed tracking graphics and data about your website. It's that simple and that profound. No other tool gives you a window into the mind of a visitor like a heat map.[24]

This information is gold. Why? Because it allows you to see what every, single visitor does when arriving on your website. No other tool can accomplish this. It's almost a digital, godlike ability, because you can't be everywhere in the world over time when visitors come to your website. It's as if you're visiting your

24 Roberts and Zahay, Ibid., 325.

website with each individual that stops by and sitting down with them as they check out your site. A heat map leaves a clear, digital bread-crumb trail of where they clicked and scrolled. Heat maps show that over 50 percent of visitors first go to text rather than a graphic when initially viewing a page. Crazy Egg and Clicktale are two of many such heat-map products you can sign up for online.[25]

The only substitute for a heat map would be you actually sitting down next to visitors, live, and observing where they click and what they do. But even doing that would make it hard to remember and manually record each click. To get results from the live approach, all you need is fifteen people, yet the simple fact that you're watching and observing could affect their choices.[26] With an anonymous heat-map tracking service, you're watching them act naturally. No pressure.

What heat maps will also tell you:

- New vs. returning visitors.
- Referral sites.
- Search terms used to find your website.
- Search engine used to find your website.
- Country the visit came from.
- Operating system used on the PC or device used to locate your website.
- Browser used.
- Day of the week the visitor found your site.
- Time of day the visitor arrived on your website.

---

25 www.crazyegg.com; www.clicktale.com, and www.attentionwizard.com.

26 Jakob Nielsen recommends only five to fifteen people for usability tests. Any more, and you face diminishing returns on your findings. http://www.nngroup.com/articles/card-sorting-how-many-users-to-test

- Google Campaign, such as AdWords, used to direct traffic to your website.

Heat maps are fun. They're simple. It's a picture that indeed paints a thousand clicks about your website. I can't describe how fascinating it is to see what visitors do when they get to your site. Best of all, the map allows you to make changes and see results.

Thank you, heat map.

Top of the fold is gold

Heat maps will also show you what part of a page is most popular, or viewed the most. Think vertical. Think vertical in quarters, such 25 percent, 50 percent, etc. For example, the top 25 percent of a page is called the "top of the fold." It's the top quarter of a web page and is also called “The Golden Triangle.” Since a visitor cannot see the entire page on most screens, for sure they’ll see the top quarter. They have to scroll down to view the remaining content and images.

That top 25 percent is gold. It’s by far the most popular section of a web page because most visitors don’t take the time to scroll to the bottom. With a heat map, the most popular page sections show up as yellow. The brighter the color the more valuable the digital real estate. In short, put your most important content at the top. If the top gets their attention, the visitors might scroll downward, but there’s no guarantee. Once the visitor lands on a page, that five- to ten-second attention window opens at the top 25 percent.[27]

Make it count. Don’t make the visitor work.

Top of mind is top of fold. Top of fold is gold.

Always, always put your Homepage value proposition and benefits statement at the top of the fold. Always put your most important **Buy** button or CTA section in the top 25 percent. Assume 75 percent of each page will be ignored. In most cases it is, thus make the top 25 percent count. Rarely ignore this rule.

---

27 http://www.nngroup.com/articles/the-need-for-speed

The "F" pattern explained

The "F" pattern describes where our eyes go when they arrive at a web page. Visitors typically scan in a pattern that's the shape of a capital letter F. Note that I say scan. Online, humans scan more than they read. In the rush for time we need the information quickly so we rapidly scan before intently reading. If we find what we want, we may shift to a more in-depth reading mode.

Think of the F shape. When humans arrive at a website page, we start in the upper left hand corner and then scan across from left to right. We then shift down a bit and continue the left to right pattern. If you apply the F pattern to the top-of-the-fold concept, one quickly sees how the top 25 percent of the left to middle of a web page is critical. If the purpose of your page is not within this area, you've missed your opportunity.

Remember that the left-to-right F pattern applies to languages that read left to right. For websites in languages that read right to left, such as Hebrew, Arabic, or Syrian, reverse the F pattern.

Usability at work

Usability means that a website visitor doesn't have to think or work to navigate each page on your site. It's natural. It's intuitive. There's no confusion about where to go and what to click. No maze. No mystery. All is found quickly and easily with little effort. Remember, visitors have lots of websites to choose from. They have also spent time on many sites. On a percentage basis, much of their online time will not be at your site.

Remember the five- to ten-second rule? The more usable a site is, the faster visitors get what they want. If they get what they want quickly, chances are they stay because it gives them more time for discovery. If they find what they want quickly, maybe they are thinking, *Hmm, what else do I need?*

The master of usability

The best tips for usability are found in the brain of one of the world's foremost usability experts, Jakob Nielsen. To be more specific, they are naturally found at his website and in the international seminars he gives. There is no better source for what works on a web page.

Below are his top twenty-five tips for home page usability. These are not guesses. These are proven and tested best practices. In fact, he has hundreds of these but you'll get the picture in the first ten. These are abbreviated and you'll have to go to his website to get all 113, and more.[28] I give all credit to Dr. Nielsen and say thanks for his wisdom and expertise. This list is abridged, so you'll need to visit the Nielsen website for more detail:

1. Show the company name and/or logo in a reasonable size and noticeable location.
2. Include a tag line that explicitly summarizes what the site or company does.
3. Emphasize the highest priority tasks so that users have a clear starting point on the Home page.
4. Clearly designate one page per site as the official home page.
5. On your main company website, don't use the word "website" to refer to anything but the totality of the company's web presence.
6. Design the home page to be clearly different from all the other pages on the site.
7. Group corporate information, such as About Us, Investor Relations, Press Room, Employment, and other information about the company, in one distinct area.
8. Include a home page link to an About Us section that gives users an overview of the company and links to any relevant details about your products, services, company values, business proposition, management team, and so forth.
9. If you want to get press coverage for your company, include a "Press Room" or "News Room" link on your home page.

28 http://www.nngroup.com/articles/113-design-guidelines-Homepage-usability

10. Present a unified face to the customer, of which the website is one of the touch points rather than an entity unto itself.
11. Include a "Contact Us" link on the home page that goes to a page with all contact information for your company.
12. If you provide a "Feedback" mechanism, specify the purpose of the link and whether it will be read by customer service or the webmaster, and so forth.
13. Don't include internal company information, which is targeted for employees and should go on the intranet, on the public website.
14. If your site gathers any customer information, include a "Privacy Policy" link on the home page.
15. Explain how the website makes money if it's not self-evident.
16. Use customer-focused language. Label sections and categories according to the value they hold for the customer, not according to what they do for your company.
17. Avoid redundant content.
18. Don't use clever phrases and marketing lingo that make people work too hard to figure out what you're saying.
19. Use consistent capitalization and other style standards.
20. Don't label a clearly defined area of the page if the content is sufficiently self-explanatory.
21. Avoid single-item categories and single-item bulleted lists.
22. To be scannable and understood, use nonbreaking spaces between words in phrases that need to go together.
23. Only use imperative language, such as "Enter a city or zip code" for mandatory tasks, or qualify the statement appropriately.

24. Spell out abbreviations, initialisms, and acronyms, and immediately follow them by the abbreviation, in the first instance.
25. Avoid exclamation marks.

After reading this chapter, now would be a good time to take another look at your website. Actually, it's best that someone other than you takes that look. I remember Jakob Nielsen saying that watching fifteen people use your site will tell you as much as watching one hundred. As mentioned earlier in this chapter, the representative sample is only fifteen. So why not do that? Videotape the sessions and study them. Then sign up for a heat map service to supplement your analysis.

You owe it to both your business and especially to your visitor. Make the visitor's experience fun, user-friendly, and value-oriented.

Don't let a visitor leave your home page with nothing. The sooner they get what they came for, the sooner you'll get a sale.

Questions and Action Items

1. Sign up for a heat map service.
2. Makes changes to your site based on what you learn from the heat map service.
3. Does your site fit the "F" pattern format?
4. Is the top of your fold gold?
5. How many of Jakob Nielsen's twenty-five usability tips can you apply to your website?

Chapter 7

MANUFACTURING WEBSITE TRAFFIC: SEARCH AND THE POWER OF PPC

"If it doesn't sell, it isn't creative."
—David Ogilvy

There are three kinds of traffic in the world: automobile, airplane, and website. Getting stuck in freeway traffic is one of the worst frustrations in life. I know—I live in southern California. You just sit there wishing you were a helicopter pilot. It burns time, productivity, and gas. It also creates frustration and stress.

Website traffic is another matter. The more the better. In fact, a website cannot get enough traffic. Good Internet marketing is all about numbers. It's a pure numbers game, and you have to drive as much traffic to your site as possible. Traffic, traffic, traffic is good, good, good. Bring it on! Tons of it.

Nevertheless, remember that not all visits are the same. It's value and not the volume of visits we must also look at. Some visits are just that: visits. Some visits lead to sales, and that's a BIG difference. Pay per click (PPC) traffic creates more sales than organic traffic.[29] Remember, not all clicks are created equal.

There are three basic sources that drive traffic to your site: direct, referred, and search. Let's talk about all three.

Organic versus PPC traffic

There are two types of search traffic: organic and PPC (pay per click). For your website, organic traffic is free; PPC traffic you buy. It's free versus paid traffic, however organic is not really free because it takes time, effort, and great SEO best practices to consistently show up on the first page of Google.

Roughly 80 percent of website traffic comes from organic searches, leaving roughly 20 percent coming from PPC. One key point: 80 percent of the clicks on a search engine results page (SERP) come from the top 20 percent of the page. The top of the SERP is prime "click estate," so to speak.

When you look at the typical SERP, the free, organic websites show up in the middle and bottom of the page. The PPC ads

29 http://searchenginewatch.com/article/2318053/The-Actual-Impact-of-PPC-on-Sales-Case-Study?wt.mc_ev=click&WT.tsrc=Email

show up in the top 20 percent of the page and on the right side of the page. On a desktop browser page, roughly eight ads per page show up. On a mobile phone, only two ads show, since there is far less screen real estate. Keep in mind that since mobile search is exploding with growth, in many cases, the only way to show up in a mobile search is through investing in PPC advertising.

In sum, the best strategy is to use both organic and PPC as a blended and balanced approach for traffic generation. Work hard to build a solid, organic-friendly site as a foundation to an aggressive PPC campaign. Firing from both barrels is best.

Direct traffic

Some traffic comes directly to your site. There is nothing in between. No bridge. A visitor, for example, just types in your URL and boom—they arrive. Direct traffic could also come from an e-mail marketing newsletter. For example, I send out a monthly small business newsletter. A "Visit My Website" link is listed under my name signature in the letter. If a reader clicks the link they end up directly on my site.

Direct traffic is good traffic because of engagement. This visitor probably already knows you and your company. There is a trust factor. They are also probably a returning rather than a unique or new visitor. Unless you are really famous and have tons of followers, direct traffic will not be your bread and butter. It's more personal and lower volume, but is still important.

Referred traffic

Referred traffic is traffic from other websites. These sources consist of links, or hyper-links, from other websites to your website. For example, your profile on the social media site LinkedIn most likely includes your business's website URL. If someone views your profile they may also click on your website link and then end up on your site. The more credible the external link, the better.

Another example of referred traffic would be my faculty profile that's listed on a local university's website. This profile covers my background information, including the URL for my company website at www.AtkinsMarketingSolutions.com. Because the local university is a credible website, this link adds credibility to my website. Think of referred traffic as an endorsement or recommendation from a quality source, provided the referral is, indeed, credible. It's a digital letter of recommendation. All the major search engines love referrals from one good website to another good website. It builds a network of credible sources.

Referred links from Facebook, Twitter, Google+ and other major social media sites are also important. It takes time to build and list these links but it's worth the effort. Get your website listed on as many credible external sites as possible. The more credible external links the better.

Search traffic

Search is king. No other traffic source brings direct, targeted, and relevant traffic to your website like search. All sources of search are important, but the power of search is second to none. I see it every day with my clients. I just cannot emphasize enough how powerful search is. It works. That blinking cursor in a search engine waiting for a question is the beginning or end of a purchase for your business.

Many small businesses are reluctant to use search. It costs money. But remember: the cost of an effective search advertising campaign is far less expensive than the problem your business faces when using ineffective, inefficient advertising. Problems such as low, irrelevant website and walk-in traffic can make or break a small business.

I also see small businesses spending tons of money on traditional advertising campaigns. Such campaigns are often hit and miss based on volume, hope, and a prayer. It's often like throwing Jell-O on a wall and hoping it will stick. If you think about it, much of traditional advertising is a hopeless volume game. You're trying to find customers rather than helping customers find you. You're pushing volume rather than letting customers pull their interest to your business.

I once had a client who sent out 3,000 mailer cards over a six-month period and only got one new patient. In less than four weeks after starting a Google AdWords campaign, he got six new patients. Search works. Sometimes it's quick and sometimes it takes time. Either way, it's still far more efficient and focused than the traditional volume approach.

For your business, search will:

- level the playing field.
- turn Google, Bing, Yahoo, Ask, and AOL into your website's personal sales force.

- transport a customer's interest immediately to the landing page of your website.
- bring the conversation going on inside the head of a customer to your website.
- turn curiosity into revenue.
- turn a need question into a product answer.
- turn flat sales into growing sales.
- match your best customers to your business.
- measure the results of your advertising campaigns.
- reduce wasted advertising dollars.
- save both you and customers time.
- make sense.
- make cents—lots of them.
- turn cents into dollars.

Search directs specific traffic to your website from people seeking your products and services in the *very moment* of their interest. They click when their interest is hot. It's the moment of interest blended with a click to action. The searcher has one goal: to get off the search page as fast as possible and on to a relevant website. Unlike social media, searchers don't "hang out" on the Bing or Google search page. The faster they get what they want, the better. The click is the purpose, not an interruption. They are already in "find mode" and "buy mode."

Search is classic pull marketing. It's giving customers what they're asking for. Like Dell's build to order (BTO) system, the customer initiates the process. You don't have to "build it and hope they will come." They already "want it and will click it."

Who are the PPC players?

There are currently six players in the global search market:[30]

- Google: 53.74 percent
- Baidu: 31.32 percent
- Bing: 10.81 percent
- Yahoo: 3.52 percent
- AOL: 0.15 percent
- Ask: 0.07 percent

The numbers speak for themselves. Google is the king of search. However, the other players should not be ignored. The average cost per click (CPC) is much lower with Bing (sometimes in the 35 percent to 78 percent range, depending on the category), yet the total reach is limited compared to Google. Google will give you more impressions and a higher click-through rate (CTR). On the other hand, the Yahoo Bing Network includes less competition for ad position, so your business may get more exposure in certain markets.

What is search?

Search is simple and complex. There's a lot we don't see that goes on behind the scenes of search engines. Let me attempt to describe the process in simple terms.

As mentioned before, search is the conversation going on inside the head of a person looking online for a product. Keywords

30 http://www.netmarketshare.com/search-engine-market-share.aspx?qprid=4&qpcustomd=0

and phrases are the language that communicates to the search engine where they want to go. The blinking cursor in the search box is waiting for words. "Tell me what you want?"

And how often does this happen every hour of every day? Lots. The following stats from Search Engine Land tell it all:

- 34,000 searches per second happen on Google
- 2 million per minute
- 121 million per hour
- 280 million per day
- 88 billion per month[31]

31 www.searchengineland.com

Remarkably, the above numbers do not include Bing or Yahoo!

Consequently, take all the millions of searches and think about what all the search engines do with this information. It doesn't simply end up in a digital black hole. It's a continuous process.

Search breaks down into two parts: searches and sites. All the searches are saved and indexed into databases that organize and make sense of all these "conversations." Algorithms, or highly advanced computer programs, take these phrases and search records and patterns, learn from them, and then add relevant keywords and phrases to their databases. In short, search engines learn the language of what people are looking for via typed words and phrases. That's the search part.

The second part is the site—websites. Advanced search engine programs, called "crawlers," scan and track websites by category and topic. These crawlers then index these websites. Because all major search engines index millions of websites, over time, this creates an organic map covering the content and category of each website. These website indexes are then used to find matches on the search end of the process.

For example, if I type in "marketing consultants," the search engine matches that phrase to relevant websites it has indexed or crawled in the past. The crawled websites make up all the organic data included in those websites. If your website is SEO friendly, as already discussed, it's easier for a visitor to find your website. The distance from point A (the search) to point B (your website) is much closer and faster, and hopefully on the first page of the search. If the search engines have found your site, the searcher can find your site. Your organic content listings on SERPs are free, provided you've taken the time and effort to create a content-filled website that's been around for at least six to twelve months.

How search is evolving: The semantic web

The Internet as we now know it is in its third edition. The first edition was Web 1.0, or what has been called the "read-only" web. It's a place just to get information. The second edition, Web 2.0, is what's been called the "read-write" web. Blogs and the sharing of content is a good example. Consumers create content by participating in and sharing it. And Web 3.0 is now being characterized as the "portable-personal" web. The mobile Internet is changing the way we interact with the web, both in space and time.

As search engines release algorithms, such as Google's Penguin, Panda, and Hummingbird, the concept and process of search evolves and changes. Search is moving toward what's called the "semantic web." It's beyond Web 2.0, into the realm of Web 3.0, and then some. In fact, the new fall 2013 "Hummingbird" algorithm is the biggest change to Google search since 2001. Hummingbird is the beginning of a more semantic search process. Let me explain.

The semantic concept of search goes beyond keywords by digging down to the meaning behind the search itself. It's the context and meaning of the search instead of the mere definition of the words used in the search. It's the contextual *Why* behind the words and not just the keywords or keyword categories. It's the meaning behind the words and not just words themselves. Foundationally, it's the search engine's attempt to understand such meaning. In short, the Google search engine is seeking to understand the meaning of web pages and not just the words of web pages. The Google preview tool is a good example. Now, when you type in the Google search bar, it attempts to "fill in the blanks" for you. It's thinking ahead for you. It's anticipating the intent or meaning behind your search string.

John O'Connor, president of JSO Digital, summarizes it well when he says, "The takeaway is not that keywords are irrelevant, but that they're no longer as segmented as they used to be. It's the meaning race now, not the keyword race."[32] Conversational search is another way that Google's new Hummingbird is being described. The search engine takes every word in a spoken question or phrase and attempts to place it in a more accurate context. It's not just a word-to-page approach; it's a meaningful conversation connected to a meaningful page. The full search string or question seeks a full web page that matches the context of meaning rather than just keywords. Keywords will always be important, but they have their limitations. It's like saying, "Nice house," instead of saying, "That's a large, beautiful, two-story home that's located near quality schools, shopping centers, and parks." Without the full context of the description, one misses out on important nuances of meaning.

Mobile smartphones are also a key part of the semantic web. If you add GPS, location-based factors, plus social media, you have an even greater context for a semantic search to draw from. Mobile will revolutionize the Internet because it's an Internet in

32 http://www.jsodigital.com/hummingbird-doesnt-change-seo-fundamentals

and of itself. It's a brave new channel for marketing. More on that in Chapter 11, but I just can't resist talking mobile.

Now that you have a taste of the semantic web, let's shift back to PPC as it relates to search. If you have a new website or a static website that has not attracted search engines, there's still hope. It's called pay per click, or PPC.

What is PPC?

Pay per click is online advertising you pay for, as mentioned briefly at the start of this chapter. Every time a visitor clicks on an ad displayed on the top or side of a search engine results page (SERP), it leads to your website. You pay for each click. You pay to direct visitors to your website. But remember, these are not random visitors. They are not "spray and pray," traditional advertising volume visitors. They are visitors already searching for the products your business offers. You don't find them, they find you because they're already looking. Your product is on their brain. Your ad is helping, not heckling potential customers. It's like asking for directions. People need a map. They know what they're looking for. PPC leads them to the right place—your website. And it leads them there in the very moment of their interest. They ask and PPC delivers.

The price for a click depends on the value of the keywords and key phrases typed to search for your product or service. Normally, there are roughly ten to fifteen top keywords or phrases in a given product category. It's a popularity contest. Google knows which words and phrases are the most popular because it tracks them every minute of every day. Google also remembers these popular phrases and then tracks and indexes them by trend and volume. The more popular words cost more. They have a value, or better said, a competitive value normally ranking from low to medium to high competitive value.

For example, the words “dentist” and “dentists” may be valued at seven dollars to twelve dollars per click, whereas the phrase “teeth whitening” may only cost three dollars per click. Since you normally will have roughly ten to fifteen top keywords configured in a PPC campaign account, Google and other search engines, such as Bing, will average the cost of those words. An “average cost per click” is determined and you are thus billed each time your ad is clicked on as it shows in a SERP (search engine results page).

It’s also important to know the difference between an impression and a click. An impression means your ad showed up on a search page. It may not have been clicked on, but it still showed up. Your business got free brand exposure and awareness. It’s not unusual over time to get thousands of impressions. The actual CTR (click-through rate) is calculated by dividing the number of clicks into your impressions. If your ad showed up one hundred times in a given day and you got two clicks, that would be a 2 percent CTR. You only pay for clicks, not impressions. In traditional advertising, you pay for every impression.

Manage your PPC account carefully

Just like your business or personal bank account, in PPC you have to manage your account spending. Cost can increase quickly if you don’t set and carefully manage a daily budget limit.

Pick good keywords and write good ads. Delete negative keywords that waste your clicks. If some days generate far more clicks than other days, don't run ads on off days. Watch and tightly manage your filters and bid amounts. Don't run ads in geographic locations that may not fit your target customer. And watch seasonal factors that could also dampen the impact of your PPC campaigns. Make every dollar count.

PPC in action

One of my clients, a dentist, had a problem: low volume website traffic. As a result, his practice was suffering. New patient growth was flat. Traditional mailers were not working and he needed to do something. Fast.

I setup a Google AdWords account and campaign. I did the keyword research, ad creation, and fine tuning needed to optimize the campaign for mobile, tablet, and PC devices. I also fine-tuned the ads and keyword search data as CTR results came in. The data tell me which ads work and which do not. I then tweak and modify for a higher click-through rate. You get feedback within twenty-four to forty-eight hours. Actionable feedback. No traditional advertising tools can touch this advantage. Not even close.

Within one month, the AdWords campaign brought in six new patients and his website traffic had increased over 800 percent. The campaign targeted eight local cities within a ten-mile radius. Simple, four-line text ads started running in these eight cities, designed for mobile, tablet, and PC devices. I also made sure the client's website was a responsive design so potential new patients could click and call these ads on either their mobile, tablet, or PC devices. On smartphones, the ads even showed a call extension so all a visitor had to do was tap on the ad phone number icon to call the dentist's office.

The ads were simple, three-to four-line text ads. There's no need for fancy graphics and images for PPC ad campaigns. Those fancy graphic ads remind users of banner ads and they often ignore them. Text rocks. As humans, we think, type, and search in text or words. Text ads work better because we suffer from "banner blindness." We see a banner online and most often ignore it.

The structure of a four-line text ad

The requirements and structure of a four-line text ad are:

- Twenty-five characters or less (including spaces) for the first line, or title/tag line.
- Thirty-five characters or less for the second line, and this line usually includes a feature or a benefit or both.
- Thirty-five characters or less for the third line, which usually includes a benefit or a feature plus a call to action, such as "Call Now" or "Learn More."
- The fourth line is your website URL/landing page the searcher goes to when your ad is clicked.

The ad below is an actual Google AdWords ad for my dental client. It appeared as the first ad when the phrase "Anaheim dental implants" was entered in the Google search bar:

Anaheim Dental Implants
One of the Most Experienced Implant
Dentists in Orange County, California
www.dentalsite.com

The website URL was changed to protect the innocent. If you have a cavity and need a dentist, sorry.

AdWords brought in business the first week, and it kept coming for this client. No other online tool directs targeted, specific, and relevant traffic to your website like a search-based PPC campaign. Bing, Yahoo, Google, and most of the major search engines offer PPC services. If you want traffic fast, go PPC.

Again, there is no substitute for a quality PPC search ad campaign. In essence, your small business becomes its own micro ad agency. You control the daily ad budget so you know what you're spending. You learn which keywords get the most clicks and then can back-end those keywords into your website page content. Also, you can even use those keywords with traditional marketing material, such as brochures and flyers. Keywords that work online may also resonate offline with potential customers.

Ad extensions

A Google ad extension is an ad format that shows extra information within your ad. Viewers can click on the extension to make their ad experience easier. These extensions don't cost more. For example, the most popular extension I use for my clients is the call extension. This extension inserts a call button into the ad.

It looks like a little phone icon. So when searchers see an ad on their mobile phones, all they have to do is touch the phone icon and it automatically calls the business for them. For businesses that depend on phone calls for appointments or customer connections, this increases both customer engagement and conversion rates.

Here is a partial list of ad extensions:

- Apps
- Calls
- Locations
- Reviews
- Sitelinks
- Consumer and seller ratings
- Social extensions

Remarketing

Google's remarketing feature in AdWords allows you to show ads to people who visited your website in the past. If they leave your website without buying anything, remarketing, also known as ad retargeting, lets you reconnect with them by showing ads when they browse the web. This also applies when they use mobile apps and when they do future Google searches. To engage remarketing, Google provides you with a small line of code that you add to the footer of your pages. Over time, remarketing is a great way to take your PPC advertising to the next level.[33]

33 https://support.google.com/adwords/answer/2454000?hl=en

PPC and preroll video ads

In addition to using extensions, integrating videos in your PPC search campaigns is another effective advertising tool. Your video previews when YouTube viewers are watching other relevant videos. It's called a preroll video. If you have a one- to two-minute video about your business, it can quickly lead to effective website traffic. You also get specific analytic reports regarding your video views.

Bottom line: create a YouTube channel and have a few one- to two-minute videos produced that tell your company and product story. Add these to your PPC campaigns so both text and video ads are directing relevant traffic to your website. Short, targeted videos are far more effective than banner ads. Pay the money for quality video production—you'll tell your business story plus attract relevant traffic to your website.

Videos are viewed on phones, tablets, and PCs. They go where people go, represent the short story of the twenty-first century, and are a fantastic advertising tool to capture and hold the attention of potential customers looking for your products. The combination of both quality text ads plus videos is an unbeatable advertising combination. Furthermore, purchase intent is also strong among those who view preroll video ads.[34]

No search, no success. Find new customers at the very moment they're looking. It's timely interaction rather than irritating interruption that counts.

---

34 http://www.emarketer.com/Article/Where-Digital-Video-Ads-Have-Consumers-Attention-Smartphones/1011322/1

One final thought. I don't believe that traditional forms of advertising will not or cannot work. They still can, especially if complemented by digital advertising. Both can work together. Just keep in mind that if you need quick, consistent, and targeted traffic, there is no better tool than an effective PPC search campaign. It cannot be beat for specificity, speed, and an efficient spend of advertising dollars.

Questions and action items

1. Practice writing four-line text ads: twenty-five characters or less for the first line; thirty-five characters or less for the second and third lines, plus a call to action. The fourth line is your URL.
2. Look at text ads on the Google, Bing, and Yahoo SERPs.
3. Critique the text ads you see on the SERPs.
4. Watch some YouTube videos on Google AdWords.
5. Is your business using PPC? Why not?
6. Have you considered shifting some of your ad budget over to PPC?

Chapter 8

BECOMING GUTENBERG: THE POWER OF BLOGGING

"No matter what, the very first piece of social media real estate I'd start with is a blog."—Chris Brogan[35]

I heard the admonition for two years: "Stu, you need to start a blog." I said, "I'll get around to it eventually." I just wasn't motivated until I learned the benefits of blogging as applied to a website. Blogging helps your organic SEO. A good blog is not a stand-alone tool—it's integrated into the entire website. It's not separate but one with the site. The worst thing a business can do is have a separate, stand-alone blog that's not integrated into an existing website. To do so is like dividing your best troops. You will lose the battle against your competition that does have a built-in blog.

35 http://chrisbrogan.com/if-i-started-today

One month after starting my blog, my website traffic increased over 300 percent. One year later it increased over 1,000 percent. Try beating that performance. Yes, it was a lot of work and writing, but it paid off. It can pay off for your business, too.

All search engines love blogs. Let's talk blogs and blogging—one of my favorite topics.

What's a blog?

A blog is a digital journal. It consists or articles or essays called "posts." Typically, these posts are at least three hundred to five hundred words in length and are focused, practical, value-oriented, and informative. They get to the point fast and should offer take-home nuggets that help your reader.

A blog structure consists of a title, main body, and sometimes a video, images, links, and an author's signature. That's usually it. For some examples, go to my website at www.AtkinsMarketingSolutions.com and you'll see blog topics and categories on the right-hand side of my website.

WordPress and Blogger[36] are the two most popular blogging platforms, however WordPress has evolved into both a world-class website and blogging platform combined. WordPress does websites and blogging well. It's the best of both worlds.

Practically speaking, you simply write your post and then click **Publish**. Boom! You have now published your content to the entire world, or what's often called the "blogosphere." By clicking

36 www.blogger.com

Publish, your post is published on your website. No middleman, and no editor who has to approve it first. Three steps: write, edit, and publish to the digital, Internet world.

You become Gutenberg

Think about it. I mean, really, think about this. In the second it took to click **Publish**, you became a Gutenberg. The power of the written word sent worldwide in a matter of seconds. With one click, you shared your expertise with the world. No physical press. No approval process. With one click, your ideas mattered to both your customers and the world. The knowledge of your one brain became the knowledge of many.

Prior to the invention of the printing press by Johannes Gutenberg in 1450,[37] the transmission of knowledge was limited to the few. Scholars and institutional religious leaders held the limited books that were available. The common man had little or no access to printed material. Gutenberg's printing press changed all that. The knowledge of the few became the knowledge of the many. Gutenberg created the Amazon of his day.

Thus, you're a Gutenberg. The knowledge of the few is easily transmitted to the knowledge of many. You know your business and topic better than anyone else. You are the expert. With the click of your publishing mouse, your website becomes your printing press. You can do in a matter of seconds what it took Gutenberg months to do. It's a miracle, if you think about it. Click power is idea power. Click-publishing power is sales and branding power. Never before in the history of mankind has knowledge been so pervasive.

You are never limited by stovepipe editors, publishing houses, or thought-patrol concerns. Provided you create great content, add value, and offer inspiration to your readers and customers, your reach is limitless. It takes time, effort, and some basic SEO, but your ideas and brand reach can spread quickly. The very reason so many news publications are struggling now is because enough quality online content exists to challenge their past information monopoly. Granted, some content is worthless fluff. Not yours. Make it count, write often and write well. It will pay off.

Blogging paid off for two famous marketing and management gurus: Seth Godin and Tom Peters. In the YouTube search bar, type in "Tom Peters and Seth Godin on blogging," and you'll see

37 http://en.wikipedia.org/wiki/Johannes_Gutenberg

the short video. It's also on my website's blog. What's so remarkable about blogging in the lives of these two thought leaders is that they started blogging late in their careers. Both said blogging was the most significant step they ever took. Hands down.

Blogging was a milestone for two famous business leaders and innovators. This is significant. If it can change the lives of two business gurus, I bet it can change the way you think and act toward your business and customers.

The proof-is-in-the-pudding factor

Aside from the numerous benefits of a blog, it gives you a platform to establish your knowledge and credibility about your product and business. If you don't know about your product, why should someone buy from you? If you can't express in writing what makes your product different, why should people buy from you or, more importantly, take their valuable time to ponder a purchase?

Regarding content credibility, I say the following on my website:

> Large followings on Twitter, Facebook, or LinkedIn do not make a consultant worthy of your time and money. A large following does not guarantee large revenue.
>
> If you're looking for a marketing consultant, read their blog and call their clients. They should have at least fifty to one hundred posts to showcase their competence. If a marketing consultant can't think for themselves, how can they think for you?

> I consult. I write. I think. I speak. I create. I listen. It helps me become a better consultant and helps me earn your read and business.[38]

The key point I make in the preceding quotation is: If marketing consultants can't think for themselves, how can they think for you? That's the crux of the digital matter. Prove it. Give me a reason to try and trust your business. Customers buy from whom they trust and whom they like. For example, I often get calls from my website visitors who found my site, liked what they read, and then called to inquire about my consulting and speaking. If my site's content, story, message, and blog had not communicated trust and credibility, the call never would have happened. I did not have to tell my life story. The credible short-story version did it. Here is who I am, what I know, and what you need. That's it. And I've noticed my call volume increases with my blog volume. As the content grows, so do my sales. I write, I work, I earn trust, they buy.

You know your product better than anyone else. Your business is the expert on the solutions it provides for your customers' needs. Give those customers strong indications that you know both your product and your stuff. Give them confidence that what you know is what your product does for customers.

How often do you post?

Starting a blog is not enough. You have to fill it with content. Great content. Regular content.

---

38 www.AtkinsMarketingSolutions.com

It's the consistent, relevant, and value-oriented content, or, better said, quality blog posts that attract visitors, customers, and search engines. You can't post every once in a while. You have to be consistent. I recommend you post at least two to four times per month. If you post once per week, that's great and does wonders in attracting Google, Yahoo, Bing, and other search engines to your website and blog. The key is consistency.

Some of my clients start off with a few strong posts, then get busy and the momentum dies. The time I've spent writing this book reduced my volume of blog posts, but I will get back on track. Granted, it's not easy to stay consistent with content, especially when business and life get busy. The trick is to plan a content calendar and stick to it. Think the following:

- One year: fifty-two weeks and fifty-two topics.
- Twice a month and roughly twenty-six topics.
- Once per month and twelve topics.
- Once per quarter and four topics (not recommended).
- A blend of two to four times per month plus random posts when you are so inspired.

Regarding creative and random posts, here's an example. In 2012, I visited Home Depot for an emergency toilet seat run. No, I did not have to go badly but our home did need a new toilet seat. Hey, it's a fact of life we all face daily. While gazing at a wall full of possible toilet seats, it hit me: *What a great blog post on product marketing!* I quickly took a picture with my smartphone of the entire wall of toilet seats. When I got home I wrote a post entitled, "The Product and the Toilet Seat." I talked about commodity products such as the toilet seat, and about how one makes a product stand apart in a competitive landscape of many similar products. I also inserted the photo and there I had it: a simple, informative, and humorous blog post that my readers loved.

The story gets better. Two years later, the president of a toilet seat company called me and later hired me to drive his US-based marketing strategy. He read one blog post on toilet seats and then read my blog for one year. He also bought my first book on small business marketing.[39] In short, one of my largest and best clients came from one blog post! Good content creates good clients. Good clients create steady revenue.

With the toilet seat post, I turned the common into content. Lesson learned: never leave home without your smartphone. Take pictures of interesting people, places, and products for future blog posts. A picture paints a thousand words and it will also get you in the mode of "post ideas." Once you get in this mode, you'll start to notice everyday life events you can write about. In many respects, it is fun. Your random blog posts are often the best ones. Mine are and I welcome the adventure of discovering content that will help, encourage, and humor my readers. A good blog will chronicle stories every minute and on every business corner. Find them.

Also remember that you're the expert. You know your product or service better than anyone else. You know the questions

39 Stuart Atkins, *Small Business Marketing: A Guide For Survival, Growth, and Success.*

and concerns your customers have. Write about them. You also know about the problems your target market faces. Write about those, too. In sum, turn your blog into a source and resource center to delight your customers and readers. Show them you know what you're talking about. It will also save you time because they can often get answers from your blog and then they call you for the "read to buy" process. A good blog often leads to good sales.

More about the content you post

If you're at a loss for what to post, please think value. Yes, value. Value offers information your readers and potential customers need. It's free advice, tips, recommendations, and lessons learned as cataloged in your blog posts. For example, my blog is broken down into the following categories:

- Advertising
- Analytics
- Announcements and Press Releases
- Business Ethics
- Consumer Behavior
- Creative Marketing
- E-mail Marketing
- General Marketing
- Green Marketing
- Internet Marketing
- Marketing Communications
- Marketing Research
- Mobile Marketing
- Press Releases
- Principles of Marketing
- Product Management
- Public Relations
- Public Speaking
- Publishing
- Recession Marketing
- Small Business Market
- Social Media
- Story Marketing
- Stuart Atkins's Book
- The Brand Called "You"

I will add more categories over time. My topics and value reach will expand. The point is to create your categories based on your business and area of expertise. Then, start writing. Offer free, value-oriented tips and lessons learned to help your visitor. In addition, think of the questions you get from past and current customers. You know the Top Ten questions you receive about your business and products. Answer those, post by post.

Also think solutions. Which problems does your product fix? Give examples, testimonials, and stories, and write about those. Chronicle the history of your business solutions from the mind of your customers. It's a powerful angle that will grab the interest of your readers.

It's also important that you stay current in your area of expertise. My specialty is marketing. I read constantly on all topics marketing related. This helps me generate a consistent stream of ideas I can offer my readers and customers. It also keeps me sharp and forces me to articulate my thoughts on digital paper. In short, your blog becomes your digital book. You publish your book on your site rather than on paper. And who knows? Over time, your posts may turn into a book. There's a professor I work with who generated his first book from all his blog posts that were written over a period of a few years. Each chapter was a post consisting of a simple, practical, value-oriented tip.

Go through your day thinking *post*. The common, everyday events of life will trigger blog posting ideas. The pictures you take with your smartphone, the videos you see on YouTube, the people you meet, the TV shows and movies you watch, the customers you speak with, the humor you embrace each day, and the stream of everyday life and business events are the fuel of blogs. Let your business and life be the encyclopedia of your content. You just have to get into this mode of life-event-to-post mentality. Your content often creates itself. In fact, it becomes fun!

Blogging is not a chore, it's a creative outlet. Your blog takes on a life of its own if you let it. See it as a canvas you paint, a symphony you compose, or a script you write. This creative outlet is one of the most powerful tools of the digital world. Take full advantage of its strength. It will take discipline, consistency, and effort. The rewards are many and will come to those who embrace blogging.

Tips to make your blog stand out

Like any marketing product or tool, differentiation is key. You have to stand out. So does your blog. Here is a list of recommended "to-dos" to make your blog move from bland to beautiful:

- Tell stories—real ones from your experience that apply to your business.
- Be creative.
- Push the envelope.
- Humor, in measured balance, is good. Use it.
- Use videos. YouTube is a wealth of blog idea sources and is complimentary.
- Use some of your own pictures to complement your posts.
- Share "How To" tips. Free ones.
- Stay away from controversial topics. Stick to your core competencies.

- Always be on the lookout for blog post ideas. They are everywhere and we often miss them.
- Divide your blog posts into categories that reflect your expertise.
- Don't be afraid to challenge the status quo.
- Draw from your experience.
- Write about a good article you read that applies to your business.
- Write about both best practices and worst practices.
- Engage your readers.
- Be humble.
- Be kind.
- Be fair.
- Be wild, random, yet half-way human.

The bottom-line benefits of a blog

There are numerous benefits of a blog, as noted throughout this book.

Here are a few more blog benefits to boost your benefit-oriented brain:

- Improves site SEO
- Increases website traffic
- Attracts search engines
- Establishes thought leadership
- Improves writing skills
- Motivates content creation
- Builds credibility
- Enhances creativity
- Simplifies website editing
- Extends social media reach
- Extends e-mail marketing reach

Remember: you are Gutenberg.

Go write. Go publish.

Thoughts and action items

1. List twelve topics you could write about.
2. List fifty-two topics you could write about.
3. Think of five stories you could write about.
4. Think of your three best client or customer success stories. Write about those.
5. Brainstorm on as many tips as you can about various topics related to your company's product or services.
6. If you're a nonprofit, tell some life-enabling and life-changing stories.
7. Find some YouTube videos that relate to your product or service. Post them in your blog and write about this.
8. Do you have existing content you could repurpose into blog posts?
9. Once you write at least fifty blog posts, register your blog on Technorati.
10. What topics do you know best in your area of expertise?

Chapter 9

DOMAIN NAMES AND HOSTING: PICKING A NAME AND FINDING A HOST

"Being a good host offsets the deprivation and loneliness of my youth."—Alan Ladd

Your domain name is your site's address and identity. Your host is where your site lives. It's that simple yet that complicated. For one computer to find another, your site needs a domain name. Sometimes you find a domain name quickly, but that's rare. It's both a process and a hassle. Some of this chapter may not be as fun as other chapters, but it's important. If you get this wrong, lots can go wrong. You can lose patience, time, and money. Don't lose patience, time, and money. "You choose wisely," said the Templar Knight to Indiana Jones as he picked the correct Last Supper cup in *Indiana Jones and the Last Crusade*.

The process of picking a domain name is like naming a child: it's not easy. You go through numerous brainstorming attempts and hope you find a domain name that matches or is close to your company name. I'm going to make this simple. Some make it complicated. That's not necessary unless your site moves into some very high-end and extremely high-volume categories and applications. For roughly 90 percent of small business sites, most of what I say should help you navigate these digital waters.

Domain basics

Computers, like humans, need names to identify each other. For a person to find a website, it will need a name. An organization called "ICANN," or Internet Corporation for Assigned Names and Numbers, manages all the domain names and registrations. Hosting companies, such as Hostmonster and GoDaddy, act as brokers of domain names so you can register and buy those domains for ownership purposes. As long as you renew your domain name, it's yours and no one else can touch it, like owning the title to a home.

This is ICANN's purpose:

> The Internet Corporation for Assigned Names and Numbers (ICANN) is responsible for managing and coordinating the Domain Name System (DNS) to ensure that every address is unique and that all users of the Internet can find all valid addresses. It

> does this by overseeing the distribution of unique IP addresses and domain names. It also ensures that each domain name maps to the correct IP address.[40]

ICANN is the standards body that polices all domain names. Most good hosting companies work with ICANN and act as distributors of domain names.

What is a domain name?

ICANN states it best on its website:

> The Domain Name System (DNS) helps users to find their way around the Internet. Every computer on the Internet has a unique address—just like a telephone number—which is a rather complicated string of numbers. It is called its "IP address" (IP stands for "Internet Protocol"). IP addresses are hard to remember. The DNS makes using the Internet easier by allowing a familiar string of letters (the "domain name") to be used instead of the arcane IP address. So instead of typing 207.151.159.3, you can type www.internic.net. It is a "mnemonic" device that makes addresses easier to remember.[41]

So a domain name is like a car license plate or phone number. The number or name is associated with an owner and it's

40 http://www.icann.org/en/about/learning/faqs

41 https://www.icann.org/resources/pages/faqs-2014-01-21-en

registered to that owner. If you have the plate, you are the owner. It's a simple way to make domain ownership traceable. In short, your domain name is the address of your website.

The naming process

Before you select a domain name, you have to ensure it's available. Often, the best names are taken, so you need to be flexible and creative. www.dogs.com may not be available but www.fundogs.com might be. A .com suffix may be taken but a .net may be available. You can also use a .biz for a business or .org for a nonprofit. A .com suffix is said to be preferable, but it's not critical. A good website that is SEO friendly with great, dynamic content will always do well no matter what the domain name. Don't obsess with this. Give it careful consideration, but remember that many of the basics I discuss in the beginning of this book far exceed the nuts and bolts related to a domain name. It's like focusing on business cards without having a business plan. It does little good and is often just a waste of time.

One other point: the length of the domain name. Short is better and easier to remember. My www.AtkinsMarketingSolutions.com is long, but still communicates what I do. One of my clients has a great domain name: www.aphmed.com. The name is just six characters. This is ideal but not always possible. Shoot for shortness but don't sacrifice the brand in the process.

Domain name and website transfers

If you ever need to transfer a domain name or your entire website to a new host, don't worry. It's common, and most hosting companies have a small service fee to do that for you. Once you purchase that domain registration, it's yours and you have the right to move it if needed. It can be a hassle and take a few days, but know you have the option.

I once had a client stuck with a low-quality host, thus we needed to transfer both his domain name and his website to the new host. After a few phone calls and e-mails, the process was completed in a matter of days. You just have to stay on top of the process to make sure all goes smoothly. This is a common process that most reputable hosting companies are good at. Just be aware that you're not stuck with a host once you move. You can fire a host and hire a new one if needed, though this can be time consuming. Pick a good host the first time and you may not have to change.

Selecting a hosting company

Hosting companies abound, and the range of quality is just as broad as the quantity. From GoDaddy to Hostmonster to iPower to BlueHost to Hostgator to A2, the list goes on and on. Many of these are fine for most small business applications, but I would make sure the following list must be covered by your chosen host:

- 24/7, high-quality tech support. This is a must. Don't compromise. Waiting twenty-four hours for an e-mail instead of an immediate phone call is unacceptable. If you cannot talk to a real person within thirty minutes, go elsewhere.
- Good customer reviews.
- Check neutral reviews from *PC* magazine and the Better Business Bureau.
- Very low downtime percentages.
- Located within the domestic United States
- Faster shared, VPS, and dedicated server options should you choose to upgrade your speed.
- SSD (solid state drive) hard drive options to make your site access time even faster.
- Dedicated IP address if needed.
- Spam filters with your e-mail service.
- Built in analytic tools, such as AWSTATS.
- Good security and firewalls to protect your site from digital bad guys and hackers.
- A proven track record.
- Automatic backup options—an absolute must.

One way to start looking is to simply Google the following phrase: "Top ten hosting companies." Also make sure to read industry reviews of hosts such as PC Magazine or CNET. Prices may vary and so will the features. Most offer e-mail accounts that are included with your domain. I recommend this. Having an @ gmail, @yahoo, or @hotmail e-mail is unprofessional. Your e-mail should echo your domain name. It reflects a real, professional company. I usually do not work with companies that don't have their domain name attached to their e-mail address.

Granted, some very high-end and very fast, dedicated hosting companies do not offer e-mail. If you need extreme speed and other factors, then e-mail hosting is not critical but should be considered. You can always have one hosting company handle your e-mail and another cover your website hosting. In most cases this is not needed but it is an option in rare cases.

The speed factor

One item of great importance, especially if your site grows: speed. Yes, speed. There is simply no substitute for a fast website. None. In many cases, small businesses can get by with standard shared hosting, but over time you may need to move to a more advanced shared hosting option that offers a faster server with fewer sites on that server, or a fully dedicated server that offers extreme speed and reliability.

For the first four years I had my website on Hostmonster, using the standard shared hosting. Then I went to what's called "Pro Hosting," a faster version of shared hosting. My server now has fewer domains on it plus it's also a faster server with a faster processor and more memory. The combination reduced the page load speed and thus improved the user experience for site visitors, especially those on mobile devices. As more and more visitors use smartphones to access the Internet, speed becomes important. Don't ignore this important factor. It's worth the extra expense. When it comes to web hosting, always err on the side of speed. When in doubt, go faster.

Ten things I learned from experience about hosting:

1. You must be able to call a human being.
2. Speed is critical. Pay more for a fast hosting package.
3. Sign up for a daily site backup service.
4. Use WordPress for your site software platform.
5. Monitor your site analytics and site traffic.
6. Use a strong password.
7. Ignore and delete all e-mails from foreign countries saying your domain is not yours and you need to pay someone to secure the domain.
8. Get notified if your site goes down.
9. Renew your domain registration and pay all hosting bills on time. Have a backup credit card on file for your host in case one expires without you remembering.
10. When in doubt, spend more time and check the customer reviews of a host before signing on.

Bottom line, do your research and ask around before you choose a hosting company. You get what you pay for, so price should not be the only factor. Remember that if your host has a problem, so does your website. If your website has a problem, so does your business. You could lose customers if your site goes down and they think you don't exist or are unreliable. Choose wisely and you'll be rewarded; choose based on price alone and you'll be sorry. All hosting companies are not equal, so do the due diligence before picking where your site will live.

Always give your website a home, sweet home to host your home page.

Questions and action items

1. Have you done extensive research before picking a host?
2. What do the reviews say about your top two selections?
3. Ask some website designers which hosts they like best.
4. Check for security breaches with hosting companies.
5. Call a prospective host to see if you get a real person.

Chapter 10

WHY I LOVE WORDPRESS

"WordPress makes it drop-dead easy to start a site. Take my advice and go do it."—John Battelle

The best decision I ever made for my company is called WordPress. Hands down. No question. WordPress restored both my sanity and strengthened my business. It drove my blog to regions I never knew possible and transformed my view of marketing in ways that are still evolving and changing for the better. WordPress rocks! It's the best. I love it. Use it.

Have I convinced you yet? If not, keep reading. If you've not changed to WordPress by the time you finish this book or chapter there is no hope for you. None. Hang up your marketing sign, close your business, and retire. That's just how strongly I feel about WordPress.

Actually, I would not go that far, but keep reading. You might just go that far.

History of WordPress

Think of the name: WordPress. You create a word then you press it. You write; you publish. It's a digital printing press for the Internet. The world. You.

As I mentioned in Chapter 8, it turns you into a Gutenberg.

WordPress was born in 2001 and was originally a blog-oriented Content Management System (CMS) software platform.[42] The WordPress website summarizes the history:

> WordPress was born out of a desire for an elegant, well-architectured personal publishing system built on PHP and MySQL, and licensed under the GPL. It is the official successor of b2/cafelog. WordPress is modern software, but its roots and development go back to 2001. It is a mature and stable product. We hope that by focusing on user experience and web standards we can create a tool different from anything else out there.[43]

Since its birth, those who use WordPress have evolved into a cult-like following and community of users and developers that have skyrocketed this tool into a remarkable addition to the Internet. WordPress has shaped careers, companies, and

---

42 http://en.wikipedia.org/wiki/WordPress

43 https://codex.wordpress.org/History

movements. It's simply the next best thing to digital bread. With butter.

Who uses it

Fanatics like me. Cult WordPress followers.

The following is a short list of companies that use WordPress:

- NY Times
- CNN
- Forbes
- Reuters
- BestBuy
- GM
- UPS
- eBay
- Sony
- Rolling Stones
- Katy Perry
- IZOD
- Stylewatch
- Techcrunch
- Samsung
- IBM Jobs
- BuzzMachine
- Mashable
- TED
- NBC Sports
- Major League Baseball
- National Football League
- Atkins Marketing Solutions

There are now over eighty million WordPress websites active worldwide—and growing. Millions of small businesses and non-profits also use WordPress. Even though it started out as just a blogging platform, it has now migrated to a full website platform that can sell up to 25,000 products.

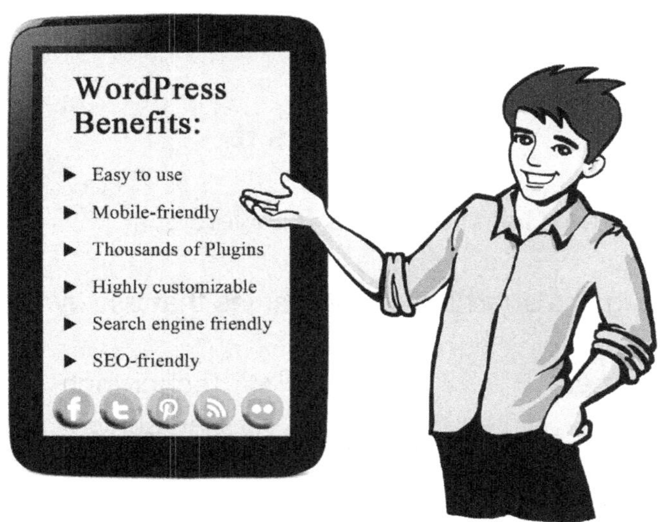

Here are a few interesting facts about WordPress:

- There are thirty-seven million WordPress-related searches per month.
- WordPress is available in at least forty languages.
- WordPress.com gets more unique visitors than Amazon.
- There are six new WordPress.com posts every second.
- There are over 33,000+ WordPress plug-ins available, and increasing every day.
- Business is the most popular usage for WordPress.
- Akismet is the most popular WordPress plug-in.[44]

Two other open source CMS platforms are Joomla and Drupal, which are more complex than WordPress. Drupal is the most complex of the three with Joomla more middle of the road in complexity. As for ease of use, WordPress wins hands down. If

44 https://managewp.com/14-surprising-statistics-about-wordpress-usage

you are looking for simplicity, SEO, speed, security, and functionality, WordPress is hard to beat. Small to medium-sized businesses fit well with WordPress. The larger and much more complex sites may find a better fit with either Joomla or Drupal.

Features and benefits of WordPress

WordPress is a content creation and management master. That's what makes it so functional—because it's born to manage content. It eats, lives, and breathes content. WordPress just loves to turn words into great websites that tell stories and run companies. It's born and bred for simplicity and ease of use. Simple is its middle name.

In addition to its ease of use, it's supported by a huge, cult-like community of WordPress fans, developers, and users. The WP bug catches fast. Once you meet a WP fan you'll know it. You instantly have a connection that bridges the digital divide. You immediately understand each other. It's almost as if you just discovered a long-lost friend.

A partial list of WordPress benefits:

- Easy to use
- Fast
- Mobile friendly
- Thousands of plug-ins
- Blog friendly
- Scalable
- Highly customizable
- Open-source architecture
- Search engine friendly
- SEO friendly
- Host friendly
- Secure
- Supported
- Easy-to-update content
- Community endorsed
- Proven and tested
- The list goes on...

Themes

A theme in WordPress is a design template. It's like picking the house you'll live in. It's similar to a magazine layout or format. Size, color, features and functionality are key. There are free, paid, and custom themes, depending on your needs and budget. Some themes are for general use and some are for custom, vertical markets, such as photographers or doctors. Themes are reviewed so select proven and tested themes with good reviews. With a good designer, many themes can be customized to fit the colors, look, feel, and functional needs of your business or nonprofit. The sky's the limit and one does not have to reinvent the wheel. I just bet there is either a free or paid-for theme that's perfect for you. If not, a good designer can create one.

For example, my wife is a nurse. She's also becoming a talented photographer. Soon we will need to have a WordPress site built so she can sell both her brand and her photos online. There are already custom themes that you can buy that are specifically designed for photographers. Her content, photos, and e-commerce pages are already set up. We just need to have a designer tweak the theme with her branding, color and design requests. The rest is set except for a few plug-ins we will add to suit her needs, such as SEO and contact info.

How's that for flexibility?

Designs and colors

Keep in mind that overall design and color themes are important to a website. Your website colors should match, in either subtle or direct ways, the colors of your company. My logo includes burgundy, black, and white colors. My website thus includes a burgundy background and black text on a white background. A white background with black text, by the way, is the hands down best choice for readability and color. Red text on a black background may look cool for about two minutes, but most readers quickly bounce from a site that hurts their eyes. Humans are used to books with black text on white or cream pages. Give them that same reading environment on a digital page.

Bottom line: simplicity of design and consistent company colors that match your logo is a good start. Don't overdesign by turning your website into a modern art fest in color. Yes, give it style, grace, and the right colors, but don't turn it into a digital tie-dye contest. The human eye and mind is calmed by simple design, minimal text, and common sense site navigation. John McWade is a master of the "simplicity, clarity, and beauty" principle, as he calls it. His site, blog, and books have fantastic suggestions for all things color and graphic related to business.[45]

Plug-ins

More about plug-ins. As I mentioned, a WordPress plug-in is similar to a smartphone ap. You download it and it's designed to perform a specific function. Instead of having to pay a bunch of money to have a website developer create the function in your site, the plug-in can be installed in a matter of minutes and you're off and running. The following is a list of just a few of the tasks that plug-ins can perform:

45 http://www.bamagazine.com

- SEO
- Contact forms
- Security
- Spam filters
- Comment filters
- Form creation
- Backup functions
- Social media sharing
- Image compression
- Caches or website accelerators
- Google Analytics dashboards
- Blog comment filters
- Ad placement
- And much more...

Most plug-ins are also updated on a regular basics so they function with newer and updated versions of WordPress. Both features and security is improved with new updates. These updates can be performed by yourself with just the click of a mouse, but be careful and always backup before performing plug-in updates. Good plug-ins are simple, efficient, proven and tested. Just make sure that before you download a new plug-in, make sure it's been around awhile and you must also read the reviews. Make sure not to run too many plug-ins, as an abundance of plug-ins can slow your site down. For most sites, around ten installed plug-ins is all you need.

This is a list of must-have plug-ins for WordPress sites:

- Akismet—protects your blog from spam
- Google Analytics by Yoast—adds a Google Analytics overview graphic to your dashboard
- Share Buttons by AddToAny—social media share button tool
- WP Fastest Cache—speeds up your website

- Wordfence Security—antivirus and firewall
- WordPress SEO—page content analysis tool to optimize posts and pages
- Login Ninja—login bodyguard with captcha to login and autobans malicious IPs and logs all suspicious activities
- WooCommerce plug-ins—lots of e-commerce plug-ins for all needed online sales orders and functions
- Gravity Forms—allows you to build simple and complex contact forms
- BackupBuddy–easily backup, restore or move your WordPress site
- Event Espresso–an online event registration and ticketing plugin

Responsive WordPress themes

A responsive WordPress theme is mobile-friendly. It automatically knows if a smartphone, tablet, or PC is viewing your website, and adjusts accordingly so the user can easily see your pages on a mobile device. This is automatic. It eliminates the need for visitors to zoom, increase the page size, or scroll to the right or left to read a page. On smartphones, a simple drop-down menu bar appears.

This is critical, since over 50 percent—and growing—of all website searches are done on mobile devices. In fact, in early 2014, mobile internet usage exceeded PC usage for the first time in history.[46] The user experience is significantly improved, and visitors can quickly find what they want without having to fight your website. They stay longer, too.

If you don't have a responsive website, you're losing business. Period. If you currently have a WordPress site that's not

46 http://searchenginewatch.com/sew/opinion/2353616/mobile-now-exceeds-pc-the-biggest-shift-since-the-internet-began#

responsive, change this now. Both potential and current customers will thank you. In short, you have to be where you customers are. Most customers are on smartphones. If your business is not mobile-friendly, your customers will think you're not friendly. In fact, many smartphone users who search for local businesses often buy within the same day. Be responsive. Be mobile.

Pick the right designer and copywriter

Choose wisely when hiring a WordPress designer. Don't pick the local high school student, or "cheap, but quality" overseas designer. Go with a designer based on references. Choose a designer with an online portfolio of past sites you can visit. Call the site owners to verify their experience. Don't pay the full price until the site is done to your satisfaction and schedule. Usually good designers require a 50 percent deposit to get started, with the final balance due upon site completion. Also, get a detailed proposal and contract that spells out exactly what they're responsible for. This way, both of you are on the same page from the start.

I do not recommend you attempt to design a WordPress site yourself. Even though WordPress is not as complicated as many website platforms, it does have nuances that favor an experienced designer and developer. It's better to become an expert in the back end, content-management side of WordPress once your site is already developed. Having mentioned that, if you want to attempt a hobby or fun site to get your feet wet, that's great. Go ahead. However, if the site is the basis of your online business presence, pay for a pro. It's worth every penny. Your time is far more valuable than money. Once you lose time, you can't get it back.

As for copy, it's a big plus if you have your website copy ready ahead of time. Since most sites are roughly five to seven pages, three to five pages of your site will be copy. Unless you're an experienced copywriter, or marketing and content development expert, I recommend you also hire a copywriter. This person should do keyword research and take the time to interview you. They must understand your customers and your business.

As mentioned in earlier chapters, less is more with website content. Make sure the content is simple, targeted, relevant, and specific as to why the visitor should buy from you, and the benefits you bring to the table. A good copywriter should be able to communicate this in the first five hundred words of your home page. If they can't, go elsewhere, or just hire me.

And finally, if you've never used WordPress, it's a good idea to get some basic training. Hire someone or go to YouTube and Wordpress.org for tutorials. As I mentioned earlier, if you can use a basic word processor, you can use WordPress. There is a shallow learning curve, and you'll learn fast if motivated. Be patient, but know this: it's fun and liberating to control and change the content of your website—by yourself. Take the time to learn the content management side of WordPress and you won't regret it.

Search engines love WordPress

Google, Bing, Yahoo, and all the other search engines love WordPress. It's search friendly. Since fresh and dynamic content gets the attention of the search engine crawlers, once they notice you have a WordPress site, they tend to come back for more, especially if your site includes content that's updated regularly.

I noticed a significant increase in my website traffic when I changed to WordPress. I also noticed an even bigger increase when I started blogging on a regular basis. In fact, moving to WordPress was the best thing I ever did for my business and website. No question.

An important word about security

Unfortunately, bad guys prey on websites. All over the world, including the United States, there are hackers who want to ruin your day, take your hard-earned money, steal your content, and crash your website. Don't let that happen. Here are some preventative tips on Internet and WordPress security for your small business:

- Back up your website every twenty-four hours. Most good hosting companies have that as a paid service. There are also WordPress plug-ins that will do it for you, too. This way, if anything unforeseen happens, you're covered and back on track within hours. Have a copy on both your PC and your hosting server.
- Use strong login passwords for both your hosting account and your WordPress login. Don't use "12345" or "Admin" for a password. Use a combination of caps, numbers, random periods or semicolons, upper and lower case letters, and symbols.
- Sign up for Malware scanning services from your hosting company or other good companies. These scan your server and not your PC.
- Update both the WordPress core and your design theme every time a new update releases. Outdated WordPress

versions are one of the biggest reasons sites get hacked. Be fanatical about this and always backup your entire site before a core or theme update.

- Have your WordPress site designed by an experienced developer and designer. Good ones build in more secure code and some even design in a firewall for added protection.
- Use only proven, tested, and reviewed WordPress plug-ins. Update your plug-ins as soon as new versions are available. Be fanatical about this.
- Beware of guest blogger requests. Never give anyone you don't know or trust detailed info about your website.
- Beware of SEO companies wanting your business and telling you your website is full of problems, errors, and low rankings.
- Use the Akismet plug-in that filters all spam that hits your website.
- Monitor the traffic and links to your site. If you notice suspect web crawlers or spiders hitting your site, block the IP address or use a plug-in, such as WordFence, to block unwanted IP addresses and countries.
- Be aware. A good website with increasing traffic is a target. Protect your digital asset with all of the above. Never let your guard down.
- If the above steps are in place, in most cases you're covered. Relax but remain vigilant.

My own WordPress story

Allow me to close this chapter with my own WordPress story. Of course, WordPress is not for every website, but in my case it was the perfect fit. WordPress took my website to the next level and it also taught me a skill to open new markets and clients for my marketing consulting business.

In June of 2008, my website went live. The designer I selected was located from a referral and the site was based on a website platform called Joomla. Joomla is a popular content management (CMS) website platform. It's robust and can handle larger websites. However, Joomla is more difficult to use than WordPress. Ultimately, WordPress gives the site user more control and ease of use.

The Joomla site worked fine for two years, but I was limited when I wanted to update content. Sometimes I had to pay my designer to update content. Frustrating. I'm not a programmer and thus I found Joomla a bit complex and cumbersome, especially from a natural SEO standpoint. To implement my own SEO best practices in Joomla, it was a chore. In WordPress, it was much easier due to the vast availability of plug-ins to help me along the SEO trail. Also, my site did not have a blog. My traffic grew some, but nothing to write Bill Gates about. The site was more static then dynamic. Traffic grew a little, but nothing substantial. My site needed attention and it was getting lonely, as I noted in the preface.

Then I switched to WordPress. The same Joomla designer and a bunch of newly converted WordPress users convinced me. Both the simplicity and the responsive mobile design impressed me. Since I'm a writer and communicator, I loved the integrated blog page and just how easy it was to create, revise, and update content and videos on either a page or a post. I was in love.

Once the blog kicked in, I noticed a big increase in traffic. I was elated. I was also writing more and blogging my heart out. I was

WordPress hooked and addicted. Best of all, WordPress started to generate revenue through increased book sales, speaking gigs, and client accounts. Over time, once I learned WordPress well enough, I created another revenue stream by training clients how to use it. It also taught me tons about SEO, SEM, content generation, video marketing, page design, usability, and security. It also taught me vast amounts of practical lessons that I bring to both my undergraduate and MBA classes. I benefited, my students benefited, my business benefited, my retirement (if I ever do) benefited, and the list goes on. In fact, it was probably the best decision I made since I started my company.

You're probably crying by now. Grab a tissue and take a breath. Get a hold of yourself.

Even better yet, the story continues.

Create your story. Start or consider a WordPress website today.

Questions and action items

1. Go to Wordpress.com, Wordpress.org, and Wordpresstv.com and start reading.
2. Google the following: "What are the benefits of WordPress." Start reading.
3. Go to www.themeforest.com and look at some WordPress themes.
4. Go to YouTube and type in the following search string: "Why use WordPress." Watch and learn!
5. Go to my WordPress site at www.AtkinsMarketingSolutions.com

Chapter 11

THE BRAVE NEW CHANNEL: MOBILE MARKETING

"I do everything on my phone as a lot of people do."
—Mark Zuckerberg

Seventy-five percent of Americans look at their mobile phone while in the bathroom. Now that's what I call "engagement marketing." The phone and the throne are now one.

The mobile revolution is here. It's changing all aspects of digital marketing, especially as it relates to the Internet. In fact, it's safe to say that smartphones have become an Internet all their own.

The smartphone is often the first device of choice for most consumers. No other device has so captured the imagination and attention of customers like that of the smartphone. Paying attention to smartphones is smart marketing. Not being ready for mobile users and traffic that comes to your website is dumb marketing. If you miss the mobile equation, you're losing sales. There's no escaping this trend. The world of the mobile Internet is exploding with growth.

Mobile is a universe unto itself. Smartphones have indeed opened a brave new marketing channel. Think of it. What you can carry in your pocket or purse gives you access to the following: the Internet, Facebook, LinkedIn, Twitter, Pinterest, e-mail, apps, music, video, TV, news, Google, Bing, Yahoo, phone calls, photos, calendars, reminders, and more. Some have called the smartphone the twenty-first-century Swiss Army Knife. That's a perfect description.

Have you ever left your home and forgotten your phone? How do you feel? Naked, right? It's as if part of you is missing because so much of you connects to your human and digital world through this device.

The case for mobile

There are tons of statistics about mobile marketing. Notice the term *mobile marketing*. New marketing is not just digital marketing, it's mobile marketing. The smartphone has created an entire new marketing channel. There is a new way to reach customers and that's through a mobile device.

Below is a list of mind-blowing mobile stats.[47] If these don't get your attention, you just don't have any attention:

47 http://digby.com/mobile-statistics

- Mobile devices outnumber humans on earth.[48]
- Mobile will pass desktop in search ad dollars spent in 2015.[49]
- Nineteen percent of people have dropped their cell phones in the toilet [50]
- Seventy-five percent of Americans bring their phones to the bathroom.[51]
- Fifty-six percent of American adults are now smartphone owners.[52]
- Sixty-five percent of US shoppers research products and services on a PC and make an in-store purchase.[53]
- Within five years, half of today's smartphone users will be using mobile wallets as their preferred payment method.[54]
- Cyber Monday sales are up 30 percent and mobile sales up 96 percent since 2011.[55]
- Sixty-four percent of survey respondents who have smartphones have made a mobile purchase after seeing a mobile ad but nearly three-quarters (74 percent) haven't received mobile ads from their favorite brands.[56]

---

48 http://mashable.com/2013/02/06/mobile-growth

49 http://www.emarketer.com/Article/Mobile-Search-Will-Surpass-Desktop-2015/1011657/9

50 http://www.cnet.com/news/study-19-percent-of-people-drop-phones-down-toilet

51 http://www.cbsnews.com/news/survey-75-percent-of-americans-admit-to-using-phone-while-in-bathroom

52 http://www.pewInternet.org/2013/06/05/smartphone-ownership-2013

53 http://www.luxurydaily.com/54pc-of-u-s-consumers-crave-in-store-digital-mobile-touch-points-cisco

54 http://www.luxurydaily.com/why-mobile-wallets-are-the-new-credit-card-mobile-commerce-daily

55 http://www.forbes.com/sites/greatspeculations/2012/11/27/the-real-winners-of-black-friday-and-cyber-monday

56 http://www.bizreport.com/2012/07/hipcricket-mobile-shoppers-buying-because-of-mobile-ads.html

- By 2014, mobile Internet is predicted to take over desktop Internet usage.[57]
- Seventy-five percent of heavy mobile users said mobile search makes their lives easier.[58]

Be where your customers are: The inbox treasure box

Your customers are on the move because mobile is on the move. With a mobile device, you can contact your customers while they're in the bathroom or the boardroom. Because smartphones go wherever your customer goes, the potential is endless. It's called "pervasive computing," because people can be contacted anytime or anywhere.

57 http://tag.microsoft.com/community/blog/t/the_growth_of_mobile_marketing_and_tagging.aspx

58 http://www.performics.com/performics-and-roi-study-49-percent-of-mobile-searchers-made-a-mobile-purchase-in-past-six-months

Think of all the communication tools that reside in a typical smartphone: e-mail, text, social media, video, search, apps, games, calendars, voice calls, and more. Did you know you can still make phone calls in this day and age? Really. Smartphones can still make old-fashioned phone calls. Don't forget that. The phone call—person to person—is still one of the most powerful communication methods around. Try it sometime. You'll be surprised when a person answers.

When talking about being where your customers are, the e-mail inbox is indeed a treasure box. Mobile e-mail has become the number one smartphone app. E-mail, being the first real social media application, has a prominent place in the world of mobile marketing. In fact most people, as noted in the preceding stats on mobile marketing and usage, access their e-mail solely through their smartphone. Perhaps the term *phonebox* will one day replace the term *inbox*.

Constant Contact, the e-mail channel service provider I've used for over five years, offers mobile-responsive newsletter templates, as do many quality e-mail marketing service providers.[59] This is an added dimension to your mobile content because, like a mobile-responsive website design, your e-mail communications also offer the optimum usability experience for your readers. There is thus digital consistency with your website, e-mail, and social media content.

In addition, Constant Contact does an excellent job coordinating all of its social media, e-mail, and event-planning tools with the latest mobile technologies and trends. E-mail channel marketing,

59 http://blogs.constantcontact.com/search/mobile+marketing/post

like Internet marketing, must stay on top of the latest best-practice trends. I give high praise to Constant Contact's product offerings, tech support, and emphasis on customer engagement as it applies to mobile trends and technology offerings. Its website also offers tons of free content and tips on mobile marketing as well as overall e-mail marketing best practices.

Think of it. Your smartphone goes where you go. It also fits in the palm of your hand, your pocket, your purse. It's a portable appendage that connects you to the world. You don't have to be tethered to a large laptop or even a smaller tablet to obtain access to e-mail. It's all there. Add to that a wearables market, with products such as wrist watches that interface with your smartphone, and additional opportunities open up.

Most people access their e-mail on their phone throughout the day. You see it all the time. Just go out in public and what do you see? Heads down and eyes locked on their phone. Always on. And because of this always-on state, e-mail is also always on and checked on a regular basis. In a sense, you're present yet absent with your customer. You are far yet close. It's not intrusion because your reader or e-mail subscriber does the choosing. It's your content on that phone that is either deleted, read, or paused for a later read. Your customer chooses which content to read, or better said, skim.

Think mobile friendly

I recommend frequently in this book the art of thinking in mobile-friendly modes. Every marketing communication you create should be a friend of smartphones, not a foe. You must think of the "phone filter" before you create any marketing campaign, article, blog post, social post, or website content. The chances are increasing every day that your content will be skimmed, read, or acted upon with a mobile or wearable device.

Here are a few practical tips:

- When writing e-mail newsletters, increase both your title and text font size to the twelve to sixteen point range.
- Be careful with large images. Less and small is better.
- With e-mail channels and newsletter campaigns, you must use a mobile-responsive, single-column template and format. Don't make readers play the horizontal shift or screen pinch game. Let them read rather having to manipulate your mobile page content.
- Reduce the amount of content you write. Get to the point and make your point.
- Use bullet points instead of long paragraphs.
- Include clickable links within the page or newsletter so readers can click if they need more information.
- Include your most important content in the top 20 percent of the "phone fold," or top of the fold. Eighty percent of your readers or skimmers will only read the top 20 percent of your cell content page before deciding to move on or stay.
- Before you send or publish content, send it to yourself on your smartphone. This way, you notice any formatting idiosyncrasies that may affect readability or usability.

Location-based marketing: SoLoMo and calls to action

Since smartphones are on-the-go devices, consumers are often moving, thinking, and getting ready to act when their smartphone is in hand. The mobile, GPS equation is critical for turning mobile into money.

What is *local search* and why does it matter to small business owners? Local search consists of online, geography-specific search tools that help to match customers to specific businesses and services. These can include Google Maps, Google Places for Business, Yahoo Local, Super Pages, Yellow Book and Yellow Pages online services, and Yelp. Local search matters because it helps local customers find businesses near where they live and work. It's convenient, and from a trust standpoint, people often like to buy in their local community.

Local search is crucial for any consumer or commercial business within a reasonable driving or delivery distance of where prospective customers work or live. If you own a retail or service business, such as a restaurant or store, a medical or dental business, an auto repair shop or a company selling residential products or services, your website should be optimized for local search.

If your website is local and mobile friendly, in a sense it moves with your customers. That's the beauty of mobile technology. It's both portable and personal. By being mobile friendly you're with your customers wherever they are. In short, SoLoMo (social, local, mobile). You ride "smartphone shotgun" next to their product and service needs.

The speed reminder

Faster page-loading speed is essential to make sure your mobile website visitors stick around. If your website does not load in five seconds or less on a mobile device, chances are the visitor will leave and never come back. Speed is a key to enhancing user experience.

On my WordPress, mobile-responsive website, I made some changes to help in this area. First, I checked the Google Page load speed test and discovered my website was loading slow for both mobile and PC devices. Just Google "Google page load speed tests" and you'll see the Google link for testing your website speed. Here are three other great sites for checking your website speed:

- tools.pingdom.com
- webpagetest.org
- gtmetrix.com

There are more speed-testing sites available, but the above three are a great start. Like the Google page-speed test, most of the others often give site-specific recommendations for how to improve your speed and fix your site. These free tools are invaluable. Run them and make the needed changes to improve the speed and overall user experience for your mobile visitors.

The hosting speed equation

Your hosting package is an easy way to increase both the desktop and mobile page-loading speeds. As I mentioned in Chapter 9 on hosting, be careful to select the lowest cost, shared hosting package. Always go with a faster server option. In most cases, a shared pro or shared enhanced version is fine. With a faster, shared server, there are fewer websites on your website's server, plus the server itself has a faster CPU with more memory.

Fewer websites means less bandwidth usage per server. Added to the faster CPU and more memory, this means an increase in your website horsepower. Not only will your visitors notice the faster page-load speed, but you, too, will notice the benefits of a faster site. Editing blog posts, updating page content, backups, and other maintenance-related functions make life easier for you, the website owner and content generator. You'll love the added speed. It's worth the extra cost—every penny of it.

Questions and action items

1. What is your mobile marketing strategy?
2. Look at your website on a smartphone. You may be surprised.
3. Is your website responsive in design, so it autoadjusts for maximum usability?
4. How fast does your website load on a smartphone?
5. Are your e-mail marketing newsletters mobile responsive?

Chapter 12

TURNING VISITORS INTO VALUE: WEBSITE ANALYTICS AND MAKING SENSE OF THE NUMBERS

"Don't expect smart people to listen to you without proof. Learn the basics of analytics and people will love you. If you don't have time to learn, hire someone."
—W. Edwards Deming

If you apply everything you've read in this book, there's a good chance you're going to get more website traffic. That's great, but traffic for traffic's sake doesn't mean much if you don't make sense of the numbers. You have to turn visitors into value.

As I work with more and more small business clients, I'm shocked that many have a website but have no idea how many people visit that site every day. In fact, I had one client that even had ten years of analytic reports on his website and had never looked at them! Not once. He had no idea how many daily visitors came to his website and what they did once they got there. A mountain of data was sitting at his disposal. This data would have been invaluable for current and future decision-making. No data equals bad decisions. It's like having money in the bank but not using it.

Don't let your free website data go to waste. Visitor traffic is a terrible thing to waste. Visitors leave a digital bread-crumb trail. Use it or lose it. Here are some points of interest and tips to help you turn web traffic into revenue.

Tracking tools: Google Analytics, AWSTATS

No matter which website platform your site is written in, you must have at least one good analytics tool enabled to track all the bread crumbs your visitors leave. This way, you know where they came from and what they did once they got to your site. Time, place, navigation, and location are critical for you to make a better website. It's a map of what's in the preferences and minds of your website visitors.

The leading tool is Google Analytics and it's free. You simply open up a Google Analytics account and Google creates the custom HTML code. You then drop the code into the footer of your website HTML code. Within twenty-four to forty-eight hours, Google will start reporting the detailed analysis relative to each of the pages on your website.

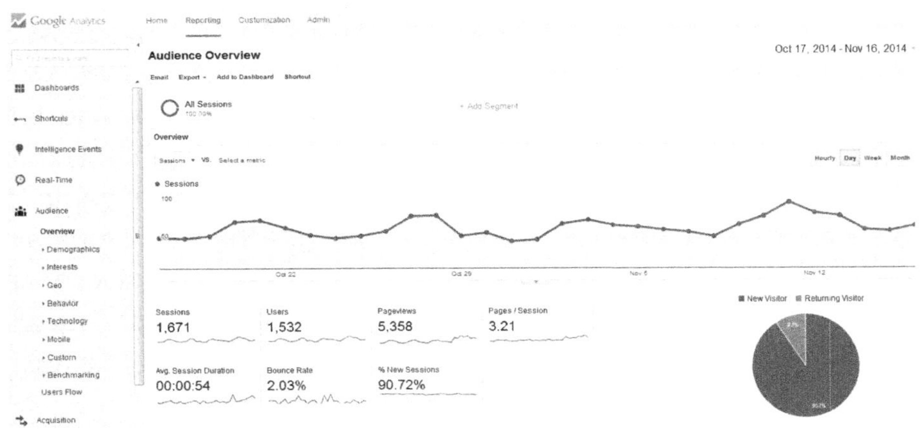

This data consists of the following:

- The number of visitors, both unique and returning.
- Page views.
- The links they came from to arrive at your site.
- The average time they spent on your site and how many pages they viewed.
- The bounce rate, or simply the percentage that landed on just one page and then left immediately.
- The type of device the visitor used, such as cell phone, tablet, or PC.
- The specific geographic location the visitor came from, such as zip code, city, state, and country.
- And more.

Another free analytic tool is AWSTATS, which is often included in the CPanel of most shared hosting platforms. Just click the AWSTATS box and save the setting. Again, within twenty-four to forty-eight hours detailed analytics will start generating reports about your visitors and their activity. Google analytics is Java

Script based and AWSTATS is what's called a log parser—it tracks traffic directly from your server's activity. There are slight differences in what each tool reports so it helps to look at both.

I used to look at my analytics reports every morning as a supplement to my morning coffee. I now look every two to four weeks so I have more trend data to track. The exception to this would be if you're running a specific promotion and want to see immediate external link data, for example, traffic from Facebook, Twitter, or Amazon that connects to an ad promotion I'm running. You can see exactly how much traffic you're getting. You can thus see which promotions are more or less effective. Invaluable.

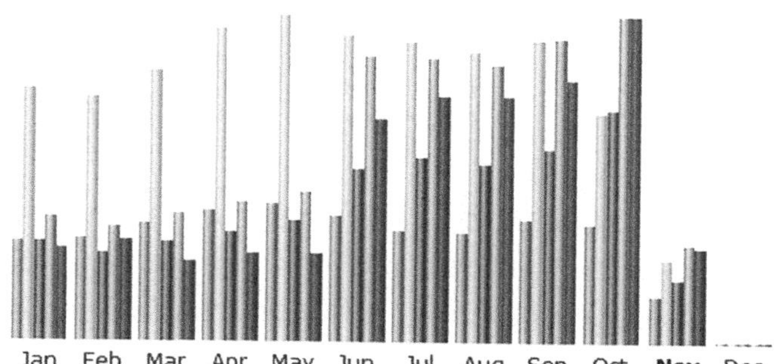

Month	Unique visitors	Number of visits	Pages	Hits	Bandwidth
Jan 2014	4,068	10,356	23,862	30,162	494.25 MB
Feb 2014	4,206	9,981	21,589	27,977	530.57 MB
Mar 2014	4,819	11,149	24,171	31,170	419.59 MB
Apr 2014	5,400	12,939	26,707	33,638	464.47 MB
May 2014	5,634	13,393	29,358	36,410	463.97 MB
Jun 2014	5,173	12,614	42,260	69,266	1.15 GB
Jul 2014	4,548	12,338	44,539	68,945	1.27 GB
Aug 2014	4,504	11,959	43,004	67,437	1.27 GB
Sep 2014	5,021	12,363	47,027	73,905	1.36 GB
Oct 2014	4,834	9,429	56,592	79,344	1.69 GB
Nov 2014	1,906	3,372	15,212	23,658	502.68 MB
Dec 2014	0	0	0	0	0
Total	50,113	119,893	374,321	541,912	9.55 GB

Note, some of the popular template-based website platforms, like Weebly and Wix, also have analytics programs to help track daily data. Weebly calls it "Statistics." Although it's not as complete and detailed as Google Analytics or AWSTATS, it's far superior to guesswork. Your site traffic needs to be based on fact, not fiction or guesses. "I'm not sure" will kill your business.

Be sure. It's the kind of information that creates sales and gives you a competitive advantage. You'd be surprised how many companies don't watch their analytics. Don't jump on the digital deadbeat wagon of missing information. Be informed.

Defining the best bread crumbs: visitors, page views, external links, time on site, and keywords

Visitors

Visitors are just that: visitors. They've shown up at the front door (home page) of your website and need something. Sometimes the visit is random, sometimes it's focused and purposeful.

These visitors fall into two categories: "unique" and "returning." Unique visitors have arrived for the first time. They're new. They may stay or never come back again. If your site is good and gives them what they need, chances are they'll come back.

Visitors that come back are called returning visitors. Your analytics tracking will remember who comes back. Those who come back usually do so for a reason—your content and products gave them what they needed. You created value and, in a sense, a digital connection, a friend who wants to come back and visit. You created an environment of engagement, or a hangout they liked. Like a good restaurant or coffee shop, they come back for more and like to stay.

Page views

Page views are gold. Page views represent a visitor who lands on a page, and stays there long enough to scan, read, and engage with the content. In technical terms, it represents the action taken by the visitor's browser. Every time a browser loads an entire page, it represents a page view. In short, a page view is a record of a visitor who stays on a page long enough to load a page, showing that you got that person's attention long enough to engage with the page content. Both new and returning visitors will generate page views.

Make sure you pay attention to page views rather than hits. Hits are a worthless metric that is often used to describe website traffic. "We got twelve thousand hits this month" is what you often hear. One piece of advice regarding hits: ignore them.

As two leading SEO experts state:

> Hits describe the number of times a request is made to your server, and page views describes the number of times an entire page is called by a browser. So if there are dozens of images on a given page, there will be dozens of hits recorded for each page view. Depending on your conversion goal, you may want to focus on the number of page views or unique visitors, but never hits.[60]

60 *Search Engine Optimization An Hour A Day*, 2nd Edition, Jennifer Grappone and Gradiva Couzin, Wiley Publishing, 2008, 150.

As noted, hits skew your data. If you have ten images on a page and someone views that page, you get eleven hits. Data gets inflated and does not tell you much.

Bounces

A bounce is a visitor who leaves your website after looking at just one page. Bounces are measured on a percentage basis, called a "bounce rate." A typical bounce rate is usually in the 20 to 40 percent range. The lower the bounce rate, the better. A low, single-digit bounce rate indicates visitors are staying on your site and looking at more than one page. They're engaged and like what they see. One of my clients with a new website has a bounce rate in the 4 to 6 percent range. That's excellent.

In addition, if a site has a high bounce rate, it may not necessarily indicate a problem. It depends on the content and products being sold. It also depends on the methods used to direct traffic to a website. For example, a company that runs very aggressive PPC advertising campaigns will usually generate higher bounce rates because the traffic funnel leads visitors to a specific landing page that may or may not engage the user. Since the focus is just a single page rather than the whole site, a higher bounce rate is usually the result.

PPC campaigns are designed to focus on a single page, then sometimes a click that leads the visitor to Amazon to buy. If that's the pattern, then higher bounce rates are common. Also, if your goal is to get the visitor to call your business and the landing page or home page clearly states, "Call Now For 20% Off," then a bounce is common because they arrive, call, and leave.

Either way, high bounce rates will often tell you if the correct target market is arriving on your site, and if something is encouraging your targets to leave quickly. It could be poor usability, design issues, a slow site, bad content, or a number of other reasons.

Average time on site

The average amount of time spent on a website tells you how long visitors stick around. Long visits indicate your site has grabbed their attention and is worth staying. If your average visit is a few seconds, you may have an issue. If your average visit is one to three minutes, then your visitors are reading and engaging with your content and products. In short, the average length of stay tells you a typical visitor's level of interest of engagement on your site.

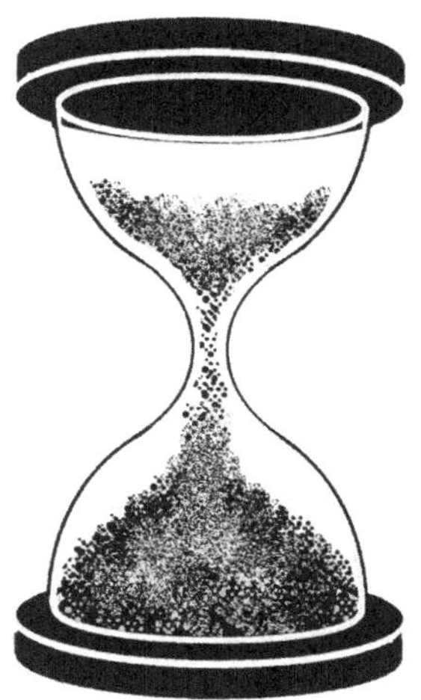

Granted, this statistic may vary with time, given the type of content and products your site offers. The focus with this metric, and for that matter all of the above analytic site measurements, is to watch trends over time. With most website metrics, it's best if you see growth trends over time.

You want increases in:

- Both new and returning visitors
- Page views
- Average time on site

You want decreases in:

- Bounce rates

The preceding stats represent quantitative measures. You also want to look at some qualitative measures, too. Here are a few.

External links

External links show the external URLs or websites where your visitors are coming from. These link sources could be other websites, social media, or other content sources. The stronger and more credible the external link, the better it is for your site ranking. For example, links going to my website from a university or a well-known company give my website credibility. An external link from a highly ranked site helps to increase the rank of my site over time. Any links from questionable or unknown site may negatively impact my site.

Digital credibility often enhances your own credibility. In the same way you can tell a person's character by the company they keep, you can often tell a website's credibility by the link company it keeps. Make sure your website is listed on the relevant sites, trade organizations, and digital entities that relate to your expertise and product or service category. Social media sites, such as Facebook, Google Plus, Twitter, and LinkedIn, are important, as are other social media sites linking back to your website.

Keywords

Any good analytic tool will track the keywords used to find your website. If you're a dentist, keywords such as "dentist, dentists, dental implants, cavities, local dentists, and teeth whitening" would be included in the keywords used to find or search for your site.

It's a must that you watch these keywords. Make sure your blog posts and key pages include both the phrases and content directly related to these words. It shows the major search engines that your site is focused on a dedicated category. It creates a natural magnet of interest by showing your site is not scattered with many topics, but instead is targeted, with specific objectives and focus.

Targeted keywords attract targeted customers. Know the mind of your visitors and customers by watching the words they use to find you. Only a good analytic tool and PPC advertising will tell you this information.

Devices: Smartphones, tablets, and PCs

Not only should you know about visitors, but you must also know which devices they use to get there. Google Analytics will even tell you which smartphone brand and model was used to visit your website.

Social media and e-mail analytics

In addition to website analytics, watch your social media analytics, too. Tools such as Facebook's Insights and Twitter analytic measurements are important. Like website analytics, social media analytic tools give you insights into what is attracting potential customers and how. Don't waste your website or your social media analytic traffic. Let them work together and complement each other. There are also numerous third-party social media analytic tools and applications that will track with even more detail. Some are free and some you pay for. Just Google "Top social media analytic tools" for ideas on what's available.

Keep in mind that Facebook's insight may have some sampling biases that small business owners and entrepreneurs may overlook. There can be hazards while traveling down the social media analytics road. Since the bulk of Facebook users are in the eighteen to thirty-nine age group, you might miss other age demographics if you're not careful. In addition, not all of Facebook's user profiles are complete, thus targeting data may not include the full demographic or physiographic market picture. Facebook Insights may give some entrepreneurs a partial vision of reality. It's a valuable tool, but be aware of its limitations.

A good e-mail marketing service provider will provide tons of useful analytic data for the newsletters you send out. I use Constant

Contact and love its reporting feature. After sending an e-mail newsletter to my subscribers, within an hour I start getting data, such as open rates, clicks, forwards, which social media tools were shared, and the times my newsletter was opened. Over time, such data tells me what works and what doesn't with my marketing communications. It gives me a window into the world of my customer—a window I always want to keep open. Most good e-mail marketing service providers offer an analytic reporting tool. If not, don't use their product. You owe it to your business to see the results of your e-mail marketing campaigns.

Make sure to combine all your website, social media, and e-mail marketing analytics together so they work in force. Once you let them all work together, each will fill in gaps you never knew existed with both your website and your business. Don't fly blind. As all great pilots do in storms or in the dark, they use navigational instruments to arrive safely at their destinations. Make sure your website gets both your business and your customers to the right destination.

Now that you've read this book, chances are you'll have a better website. But you have to act. Do something. If I could give you one piece of advice in all twelve chapters, it's this: measure your marketing. Don't let one visit, page view, comment, or mobile call go to waste. Keep track and know the trends, minds, and wishes of your website.

If you know these, you'll better know your customer. To know your customer you must win the battle for attention.

Go get your customers' attention. Go introduce yourself.

Questions and action items

1. Do you have an analytic program that tracks your daily website traffic?
2. How many visitors come to your site every day, month, and year?
3. How many page views does your site receive every day, month, and year?
4. What do the analytic trends tell you about your site over the past months and years?
5. What's the average time spent on your website over the past month and year?
6. If you have more than two years of analytic data, what can you conclude and change from these trends?

APPENDIX

Miscellaneous Blog Posts on Internet Marketing

This appendix is a compilation of blog posts I've written over the years on Internet marketing. Some of this material may repeat prior points or principles from the chapters you just read. This is an intentional "method to my Internet madness." The purpose is reinforcement, not redundancy. Read, learn, review, and remember.

How to make money online

By
Seth Godin

1. The first step is to stop Googling things like, "how to make money online." Not because you shouldn't want to make money online, but because the stuff you're going to find by doing that is going to help you lose money online. Sort of like asking a casino owner how to make money in Vegas...
2. Don't pay anyone for simple and proven instructions on how to achieve this goal. In particular, don't pay anyone to teach you how to write or sell manuals or ebooks about how to make money online.
3. Get rich slow.
4. Focus on the scarce resource online: attention. If you try to invent a way to take cheap attention and turn it into cash, you will fail. The attention you want isn't cheap, it's difficult to get via SEO and it rarely scales. Instead, figure out how to earn expensive attention.
5. In addition to attention, focus on trust. Trust is even more scarce than attention.
6. Don't worry so much about the 'online' part. Instead, figure out how to create value. The online part will take care of itself.
7. Don't quit your day job. Start evenings and weekends and figure it out with small failures.
8. Build a public reputation. A good one, and be sure that you deserve it, and that it will hold up to scrutiny.
9. Obsessively specialize. No niche is too small if it's yours.
10. Connect the disconnected.
11. Lead.

12. Build an online legacy that increases in value daily.
13. Make money offline. If you can figure out how to create value face to face, it's a lot easier to figure out how to do the same digitally. The web isn't magic, it's merely efficient.
14. Become the best in the world at something that people value. Easier said than done, worth more than you might think.
15. Hang out with people who aren't looking for shortcuts. Learn from them.
16. Fail. Fail often and fail cheaply. This is the very best gift the web has given to people who want to bootstrap their way into a new business.
17. Make money in the small and then relentlessly scale.
18. Don't chase yesterday's online fad.
19. Think big, act with intention and don't get bogged down in personalities. If it's not on your agenda, why are you wasting time on it?
20. Learn. Ceaselessly. Learn to code, to write persuasively, to understand new technologies, to bring out the best in your team, to find underused resources and to spot patterns.
21. This is not a zero sum game. The more you add to your community, the bigger your piece gets.[61]

61 Usage by permission of Seth Godin: Seth's post is a commentary about selling online that's both ironic and intentionally contradictory. http://sethgodin.typepad.com/seths_blog/2012/05/how-to-make-money-online.html

Marketing and Internet Statistics: This Site's Info Speaks for Itself

The Internet has changed marketing worldwide. Since 1996, marketing has not been the same.

The information on the site URL below will motivate, inspire, and intrigue you.

If your small business does not have a website—see this site. If your company has not revised its website—see this site. If your company does not have a long-term Internet marketing strategy—see this site. If your company does not have a social media strategy—see this site. If you believe in paradigm shifts that change forever the way we think, act, and do business, then see the site below.

If you think the Internet is just a fad and that "business is just business," well, nothing can help you. However, in that case, go to the site below anyway. The facts may just change your mind and actions.

www.Internetworldstats.com

Website Design: Do You Know Your Keywords and Phrases?

One of my neighbors owns a small residential and commercial painting company. He had a website, but few conversions were resulting from the site. I took a brief look at the HTML source code on his home page (something anyone can do) and noticed he had no HTML title pages or keywords or key phrases. His site copy was also missing keywords common to a small painting business. Even though the site looked respectable from an appearance and graphics standpoint, the HTML keywords and page titles were making it difficult for potential customers and search engines, such as Google, to find his business. I gave him some basic advice on where and how to add both page titles and keywords.

About three months later, I asked him if he'd noticed a difference. He said, "Yes, it's been like day and night!" His website was generating more leads and revenue. Potential customers could now find his website—simply because he made a few basic changes to his HTML and copy.

As my neighbor the painter says, "Just because you have a website doesn't mean people will find it." In fact, if you don't take a few simple steps, ***no one*** will find it. Sure, if people know your domain name, they can just type that in and arrive at your site. However, if they don't know you exist and are looking for a small business that provides your product or service, you have to place yourself into the mind-set of the searching customers. Which key phrases or terms would they use to find your company and its product or services? Put yourself in their searching shoes. Think,

Hmm...I'm sitting at a keyboard, and this is what I need. So what would I type in to find it?

Subsequently, the text in your website ***must*** be search engine friendly; in other words, it should be easily understood by search engines, such as Google, Yahoo, MSN, and Ask. If all you had on your website were clear, understandable text that included the ten to twenty most common words used to search for your business, product, or service, then you would be well ahead of most websites.

You can have all the graphics, bells and whistles, flash video, and music you want. Google, Yahoo, MSN, and Ask do not care about that. Text is master, and text is all the search engines understand. Without the right text in your pages and your HTML code, the search engines will not find your website or your business. In fact, did you know that Google uses the first fifteen hundred words on your site as a benchmark for search criteria? Because of this, make your text count.

For example, let's say you have a small business that sells rebuilt Chevy 350 engine blocks. Keywords in your site may include the following: rebuilt engines, engine, 350, Chevy 350, rebuilding, camshafts, pistons, water pumps, and so on.

Here is a quick way to find keywords used on just about any website. Just go to the "View" pull-down in your browser and then click "Source." The next screen that comes up will be the HTML source code for the website you're on. You can also click the right mouse button to find this.

The screen will show the keywords used in the HTML text code of the website. Words such as *business, marketing, small business*, and *recession-proof* are all possible keywords my visitors and potential clients would use to search for my site and services as a speaker and marketing consultant.

You can also pay for services that help you find keywords. A company called Wordtracker has an excellent feature set that locates keywords related to your products and markets.

www.wordtracker.com

Who Should Design and Build Your Website?

There are several choices available to the small business owner for website design, development, and maintenance. If you choose the do-it-yourself approach, be prepared for a significant learning curve. I thought at first I could get some free templates and just build the site myself. Well, it was not so fast and not so easy. I consider myself pretty tech savvy, but I quickly learned that hiring a pro is the way to go. In my mind, time is much more valuable than money. The amount of time and hassle one spends learning the digital web design ropes is much better spent on doing what you do best: running your small business. If you've never designed a site yourself, attempting this task can be a rapid net loss of time for your business.

Some companies offer turnkey, template-based websites that allow you to create, edit, and update your site in a short time. For some small businesses this may be a good starting point, except most turnkey, template-type sites look more generic than professional. If all you want is a cookie-cutter look and feel, then you can go in this direction for site design. If you choose this approach, make sure you still apply these tips to optimize and maximize your site visibility.

Once I decided that someone else needed to build my site, I looked at numerous options. There are tons of web design companies whose services range in price from $300 to $30,000. The range is just that large. So make sure you determine your web development budget. Once you have these figures in mind, you can start the hunt. The web design companies may be local, regional, or global. Since most of the development communication is done through e-mail, file attachments, and phone calls, it's feasible to work with a company across the country or the world. Just Google "website design companies" and you'll have a starting point. You can also narrow the search to your local region or city.

After talking to five different nationwide web design companies, I chose to go with a local designer because I like to outsource based on referrals from someone I know. It's also a plus if they are local to your location. A former supervisor of mine started her own company a few years back. I liked her site, so I called and asked some questions about her web designer. The feedback was positive, so I called the designer, and we discussed my needs and budget. I also asked for links to sites she'd designed in the past. I liked what I saw. Within about a week I made my decision, and we were off and running. Since I'd already written the text for each of my pages, half the work was done. I told her which sites from her portfolio I liked, and that design was used as a rough starting point. Within about one month, my site was up and running.

Don't go out and find a fifteen-year-old high school student. Hire an experienced web designer who knows what they're doing. You just cannot risk the delays and pains involved with an amateur. Because your website is such a critical weapon in your marketing strategy, don't take the risk. Furthermore, you'll need support and have questions in the future. Having a local number to call with questions puts your mind at ease.

Bells and Whistles: Special Effects and Website Design

Bells, whistles, and BS mean flash graphics, videos, and the entire range of special effects one often sees on websites. Should you use them? In some cases, yes; in most cases—***no.***

Tasteful and well-done videos are a fantastic tool to display your product or service, as well as your communication skills and expertise. Videos are almost a necessity to capture the attention of the YouTube generation. You can develop your own studio effect by creating high-quality and informative videos to post on your site.

There are a couple of options here. One is to hire a video production company to shoot and produce your videos. This can be expensive, but there are few substitutes for a professional video. Another method is to do it yourself. You can purchase a quality, high-definition video camera or, in many cases, do it on your smartphone. Once the shoot is complete, it's just a matter of transferring your video file to your PC for editing.

YouTube provides a no-cost platform to launch your videos. On my website, I often just upload my promotional videos to YouTube and then use YouTube's code insertion utility to place the video on my site. If your website is WordPress, it's as simple as cutting and pasting the YouTube URL into your page or post. This also allows you to track the exact number of views over a given time period. All you need to do is simply log in to your YouTube account, and then you can check your video view reports.

You also will need video editing software, and prices on those vary widely. Windows Movie Maker comes with newer versions of MS Office and includes tools you can use to edit and produce quality videos. Apple iMovie is another effective editing tool.

If you can take a moderate and balanced approach to special effects, then go for it. Only use them to enhance and drive home your point or product. Don't include tons of graphic bells and whistles just to be hip or with it. They must be justified. Don't be cool or fancy just for the sake of it. Less is more. Remember, keep it crisp and clean. The less the clutter, the more your message gets through. The sweet spot video length is one to two minutes. Any longer, and viewers don't view.

One tip: Always include at the end of your videos your domain name text (on screen). This way, when you post to YouTube, Facebook, and other social media platforms, it promotes your website during each view.

Looking for a Search Needle in a Google Haystack

Websites often miss a critical customer magnet: keywords and phrases. When potential customers search in Google, there are five to ten words or phrases that connect their search to your site.

A search engine acts as a middleman between customers who want something and businesses that can provide it.

Keywords and phrases are the descriptive words you want your website to be found with on search engines. Simply put: your customers may not find you if you don't include the right words in your HTML page titles, keyword meta tags, and your page content. Make sure your customers are not looking for a search needle in a Google haystack.

For example, "marketing tips," "marketing," "marketing consultant," and "Stuart Atkins," are just a few of the keywords for my website. The rest are highly classified. Only Jack Bauer knows my remaining terms.

Without such words, it's like playing "Hide and Seek" for a customer to find your business. You may have a fantastic product or service, but what good is it if no one knows your business exists? Even if your site is a design masterpiece, without the right keywords, potential customers may never find you. They are gone for good. They buy somewhere else.

Don't become invisible.

Quality Website Content Beats Page Rank Any Day

What good is a number one Google page rank if your content is weak and fails to serve the needs of your reader? Actually, if you have poor content, you'll never get a good page rank anyway.

Content is king. Relevant, fresh, current, and thoughtful content. There's no substitute. No matter what those SEO e-mails/companies may tell you about "letting us rocket you to the top of Google page rankings," there's no substitute for daily or weekly fresh content to your site.

Instead of spending money on SEO shortcuts, invest in something more valuable: take the time to write good content.

For example, for months I delayed starting a blog. I kept putting it off thinking, ***I'll get around to it.*** In April of 2010 I started my blog. I could not believe my analytical, metric, web-traffic eyes. Within two to three months my visitor traffic and page views increased threefold.

In sum, do the following before spending money on page ranks and "SEO Specials." Try this first:

- Research ten to fifteen keywords that define what your business is all about.
- Include those keywords naturally in your page content. Don't force it in a mechanical manner. Write naturally, but focus on those keywords that make most sense.

- Start a blog. Not a standalone blog, but a blog integrated into your site. Search engines love the fresh blog content. Post two to four times a month if you can.
- Use an analytic tool, such as Google AdWords or AWSTATS, to monitor your site traffic, such as page views, unique visitors, and average time on site.

The Value of a Value Proposition

Do you know your value proposition? Can you summarize, in one sentence, why a potential customer or client should buy from you? Or, as www.marketingexperiments.com defines it: **"Value proposition is the primary reason why a prospect should buy from you."**[62] You need to understand and know your value proposition.

Key Questions

- Is this value statement in the first 300 words of your Homepage?
- Is it clear and concise?
- Does is express unique value?
- Does it invoke and define what sets your business apart?
- Have you clearly differentiated your product offerings from competitors?
- In at least one aspect of value compared to your competitors, do you excel?
- Do both your company and your products have their own, unique value propositions?
- Can you answer why your target prospect should buy from you instead of your competition?
- Can you communicate the above in one or two sentences in fifteen seconds?

Your value proposition forces you to focus on what matters for your customer, not you. It zeroes in on one thing: benefits. It also

62 http://www.marketingexperiments.com/blog/wp-content/uploads/MarketingExperiments-Value-Prop-Worksheet.pdf

answers the question, "How can my product or service really impact my customer?" You owe it to both your business and your customer to know your value proposition. It's an exercise in simplicity and clarity.

Your "speed to cool," or how fast you can communicate this proposition, matters. Just how clearly and quickly you get to the value statement is critical. Many small business websites miss this. Knowing your value proposition is gold.

Here's my value proposition:

"Atkins Marketing Solutions is a small business marketing consulting company that helps you tell your story, audit your marketing, and find your customers."

Start writing that single sentence. Write it, revise it, and finish it.

Go create some value.

The Benefits of Selling Electrons Versus Atoms

"Sell electrons, not atoms."
—Bill Myers

You're reading electrons when you're online. Electrons bring you to the Internet. Electrons matter and they go beyond matter. The benefits of selling electrons versus atoms are significant.

I love the quotation above by author Bill Myers. It could not be said better. If you're in the business of selling atoms you face limits—physical products, in other words. They will always be with us because tangible is necessary when it comes to everyday life. Functionality and fashion merge on the field of necessity. However, when we speak of atoms, or information, or content, or ideas, or innovation, or apps, or websites, or e-books...the list becomes infinite. You get the picture, but it also goes further.

More and more jobs are information based. The skill becomes the ability to take information and turn it into profit. Information and content placed within the right context allows both businesses and consumers to do one critical thing: make decisions—informed decisions. These decisions make money. These decisions save money.

Take the preceding concepts to the marketing level and it gets even better. The best marketing creates and communicates the purpose of digital electrons: content. If you can create the proper messaging and content that connects with your customers, and then make sure that content is easily found online, half the battle is won. The concept of search is a pure electron function.

Electrons blended with language match customer needs to your content. Your electrons. You can have the best atoms (products) in the world but if you cannot communicate with the right message, content within context, and draw targeted customers to your website, you are not electron empowered. Be empowered. Sell electrons.

Hint: if you're reading the e-version of this book, you're reading electrons.

How to Set Up a Google AdWords Account

It's usually best to have an AdWords specialist set up your account, but for the brave and motivated of heart, you can try it yourself. I taught myself AdWords but it takes time, effort, and trial and error to see results. These are the basic steps:

1. Go to google.com/adwords
2. Click "Start Now."
3. Answer all the choice buttons.
4. Create your campaign.
5. Create four-line text ads for both mobile and PC, provided your website is mobile responsive/mobile friendly.
6. Choose your daily budget.
7. Use the setting tab to target cities, states, or countries.
8. If you want calls to your business, set up call extensions that include your phone number.
9. Set an end date or no end date for your campaign.
10. Wait thirty minutes to a few hours for your ads to be approved.
11. Start watching your results come in within twenty-four to forty-eight hours. Tweak, improve, and fine-tune your account. Be patient. Give the data time to teach you.

One of the keys is to pick good keywords, write good ads, and be patient. Use your leading keywords as part of your four-line text ads. In addition, watch the keyword performance results in the keywords tab. After about a week, you'll have enough data to start making decisions, such as which ads to refine or pause. You will also start to notice which keywords perform better. In most cases, using phrase match keywords are best. Phrase match allows for your ad to show up when there are close variations of a keyword, or other words before or after a specific keyword.

You can also call Google for help. The AdWords support staff people are helpful, friendly, knowledgeable, and go out of their way to help you. Learn from them.

Start with a lower daily budget, then increase your spend as you refine the account. Some product ad categories are more expensive than others. It depends on the category and competitive nature of your product or service.

AdWords will give you a window into the world of potential customers. Use it, but be mindful to watch your spending. An AdWords account that is set up correctly will maximize your ad dollars.

How to Do Your Own Website SEO

Beware of SEO companies that claim to "get you to the top of Google." Many of them are rip-offs, as evidenced by the numerous small businesses that have fallen victim to the black hole of SEO. I hear it almost every week as I advise small business clients ranging from start-ups to well-established businesses. Most basic best practices needed to make your site search engine friendly, and thereby draw relevant and targeted traffic to your website, can be done yourself. In fact, the foundation of all good SEO rests in the following five words: dynamic, weekly, relevant, and fresh content.

I significantly improved my Alexa ranking over the years. With time and content, I have increased my site traffic significantly. I'm not so much interested in a Google ranking as I am in seeing a consistent, growing trend of relevant traffic to my website. Here are a few tips:

- Use WordPress. Period. Let me say it again: use WordPress for your website. It's not just a content management and blogging platform anymore. WordPress does it all.
- Include a blog as part of your site.
- Post two to four times a month. Post more if you have time.
- Post relevant content that relates directly to your business and area of expertise.
- Make your posts benefit-oriented, with tips and practical information to help your readers.
- Use an SEO plug-in to optimize and improve each page and post.

- Do keyword research and integrate those leading terms and phrases into your page copy. Write in a natural, not mechanical style.
- Post your site map to all the major search engines.
- Use Google AdWords and learn from your keyword research.
- Use custom descriptions for each page of your site. Match the page title to the main content of each page.
- Link Facebook and Twitter posts back to your blog using a social media share bar with each post. There are plenty of good share bar plug-ins for WordPress.
- Use the Alexa toolbar. Go to Alexa.com to see what's available and where your site ranks. It will be an eye-opener the first time you enter your URL and hit **Enter**.
- Get your blog listed on Technorati.
- Get your site URL listed on as many relevant websites as possible. The better the external links returning to your site, the better your site visibility.
- Watch your page-load speed. Slow will hurt you.
- Be patient. It takes time for Google to trust you.
- Don't overdesign your site. Google likes sites that offer relevant content, not digital art museums that dance around like the Disneyland night parade. Again, relevant content beats fancy design any day.
- Use AWSTATS and Google Analytics to track your site traffic and progress. If you don't check what's happening with your site numbers you're flying blind. Don't fly blind.

These are just a few of my tips. Apply the above and you'll both save money and increase relevant traffic to your website.

What Makes a Good Website Home Page?

There's no place like home page.

The home page is the most important page on any website. In most cases, it's the first page visitors land on. It's often the only page they land on. It's the starting point for the rest of the site. If the home page does not deliver, the visitor leaves. If you don't get it right, they may never come back. Never. Scary, huh?

The first 300 words of the home page set the stage. It makes or breaks whether the visitor stays. It's like a movie trailer and it better be good. The following list includes the must have elements in a good home page:

- Ask yourself, "What's the purpose of this page?" One purpose.
- State your value proposition in the first paragraph, if not the first sentence.
- Include your benefits statement, listing the top three to five benefits you provide your customers.
- A short video telling the story of your business. Two to three minutes max. Professional but casual.
- Some closing content describing more differentiators about your business. Things that truly set your products apart. What is unique about your products compared to the competition?
- Include your business phone number and e-mail address at the top of the page fold, easily visible.

- Be careful about tempting visitors with links to other pages of your site. Keep them on the page and be careful about including distractions.

And remember—get to the point with short, active (not passive) verb sentences. Don't attempt to include your entire company story or descriptions of all your products or services. Leave that for other pages or blog posts, but please don't flood the visitor with too much information. They can't drink from a fire hose of content. Sipping is best.

The home page is the first step in the journey of a thousand page views. Make it count.

The Critical Website Question: "Why Am I Here?"

Do you know what the most important website question is? "Why am I here?" Your site visitors ask this question every time they show up. It's critical, and after Seth Godin mentioned this question in a blog post a few months back, I just can't stop thinking about it.

It's hard to create success if you're not present. But why did you show up for a digital visit? Ask yourself why people visit your website. What's the answer? Here are a few:

- I'm bored.
- I found this site by accident.
- I'm looking for your expertise.
- I need help in your product or service category.
- I'm a hacker.
- I'm a spammer.
- I make "money" by bothering websites.
- I'm a bot bum and have nothing better to do.
- I need to do something.
- My business is suffering.
- I need to see what my competition is up to.
- I like good content.
- I like to learn.
- I need to buy a service or product.
- I need information.
- I need to grow sales.
- I need to understand my customers.
- I don't know.
- I sell links.

- I steal others' content without permission.
- I know you.
- I heard you speak.
- I read your book.
- I took your class.
- I need marketing help.
- You fill in the blank: ______________.

Let Your Website Create Brand Awareness

In essence, a brand is a promise. Your potential customer needs a solution, and your product promises to provide that solution. Yet a brand goes far beyond just a logo or a tag line or a name. A good brand has consistency of color, design, and most importantly, messaging. You have to tell your story and the story can't be told unless you spread the word. A good website spreads the word like no other tool because you don't have to shout to get people's attention. They search and find you rather than you shouting to interrupt them. Often, the customers find you before you find them. How? Search. Internet search.

In many cases people find companies and products by a simple Internet search. They type in a keyword or phrase, hit **Enter**, and the Google page does the rest. If your site is visible and has caught the attention of the major search engines, chances are a potential customer may become aware of your brand and company simply through an Internet search.

Some of my best clients, speaking gigs, and radio interviews found me from my website. I did not seek them—they sought me, or better yet, found me. It was pull marketing created by digital brand awareness. If your website is search friendly, your brand will be friendly. If they can't find you online, they don't know you exist. Scary but true. Your brand's awareness is often dependent on your website's visibility. If your website is not on the radar, your brand won't be on the radar. If a potential customer can't find you, how can they buy from you?

Be found.

Website Legal Issues

The protection of intellectual digital property is important for your website and for your customers and clients. Online abuses are many, so be careful. I'm not an attorney. Make sure to check with a lawyer familiar with online digital property rights just to make sure.[63] Bitlaw.com covers many topics also.[64] Online legal sites are not a substitute for professional legal advice.

Here are a few things to consider:

- Keep your website copyright date current on the footer of each page.
- Make sure to include a Terms of Service agreement on your website if you plan to sell online.
- Don't copy and paste images or photos from other websites and then use them on your website. You must have either full written permission, or you must purchase the license rights to use online photos or images.
- In blog posts, always give credit to whom credit is due.
- Be careful with fair use and public domain laws. On your website pages or blog posts, if you quote another source, do so in limited fashion and include a link to the full text or article.
- Any PDF files you post on your website can (and in many cases will) end up on some website you've never heard of. You can't control all your online content, so know that your PDF files are low-hanging fruit for content thieves.

63 Wikipedia has a good article covering the basics of copyright issues: http://en.wikipedia.org/wiki/Wikipedia:Copyrights#Guidelines_for_images_and_other_media_files

64 http://www.bitlaw.com/Internet/webpage.html

- If you've purchased your domain name through a legitimate source, such as your hosting company, you own that domain name. If you ever get an e-mail claiming that you have to pay someone $399 to fully protect your domain name because it's used overseas, ignore the e-mail. Delete it. It's a scam.
- Again, always check with an intellectual and digital property rights attorney regarding your website issues. In an abundance of caution, when in doubt, get a professional legal opinion before putting anything online.
- It's a wild, wild digital world out there. Be wise. Be protected.

Tips for Selling Online

If your product is shipping-ready and fits the e-commerce model of selling online, there are important things to consider before opening up your online digital cash register. An e-commerce site has nuances and issues that go beyond that of the typical, information-type website. Since most of my e-commerce experience is with WordPress, I will speak from that context; however, many of the following tips apply to other e-commerce platforms.

Here are some practical tips and considerations:

- Think of the entire buying and selling process, from the landing page and shopping cart, to the credit card transaction, to the shipping and tax bracket by state selection and setup. You must cover all of these.
- Use an e-commerce plug-in or tool that integrates with your accounting software, such as QuickBooks.
- WooCommerce (www.woothemes.com/woocommerce) offers accounting, import and export, payment gateways, products, reporting, shipping methods, tax rates by state, and subscription plug-ins and extensions.
- Have simple and clear product buy pages with pictures and bulleted descriptions of your products.
- Visit websites that do e-commerce well. Note how they streamline and simplify the process. Model those examples.

- Make sure to include a Terms of Service agreement on your website if you plan to sell online. Since online financial transactions include storing personal information, you will need such an agreement. There are some online you can view as templates.
- Purchase a Secure Sockets Layer (SSL) certificate. An SSL certificate encrypts information sent to the server using SSL technology. This protects credit card information and ensures the privacy and protection of e-commerce data used during the buying and selling process. It makes website transactions secure. It's usually an annual subscription purchased through your hosting company.
- Use e-commerce plug-ins that allow integration with the Amazons of the world so you can also refer your website traffic to other online vendors on which you may offer your products.
- Amazon example: I sell my books on Amazon using a print on demand (POD) model. None of my books are printed until an order is placed on Amazon. I use PPC advertising to direct traffic to my website's book landing page. This page offers descriptions of my books in addition to an Amazon **Buy** button. Once my website visitor clicks on the **Buy** button, Amazon handles the rest of the transaction. Keep in mind that online distribution channels like Amazon take a percentage of your sales transaction as a service fee.
- Sell both direct and through third-party online distribution channels to maximize your reach. This choice depends on your product line and your infrastructure for direct online selling and shipping from your location.

- Make sure buyers can easily contact you through both an on-site contact form and by phone. Be available.
- Ask for permission to collect buyers' e-mail addresses so you can stay in touch and send e-mails about future offers.
- As Seth Godin says about selling online, "Get rich slow."

ATKINS MARKETING SOLUTIONS

- Visit my website and blog at AtkinsMarketingSolutions.com
- Send me an email at stu@atkinsmarketingsolutions.com.
- Follow Atkins Marketing Solutions on the Facebook page called “Atkins Marketing Solutions.”
- Follow Stuart Atkins on Twitter & LinkedIn.
- For monthly marketing tips, sign up for my e-mail marketing newsletter on my website.
- Hire Stuart Atkins as your marketing consultant.
- Hire Stuart Atkins as a speaker.
- Read my first book entitled, “Small Business Marketing: A Guide for Survival, Growth, and Success,” which is available on Amazon.

Notes

Notes

INDEX

Made in the USA
Columbia, SC
20 September 2021

45621382R10114